CREATIVE
HOMEOWNER®

design ideas for
Home Storage

CREATIVE HOMEOWNER®, Upper Saddle River, New Jersey

COPYRIGHT © 2006

CRE▲TIVE
HOMEOWNER®

A Division of Federal Marketing Corp.
Upper Saddle River, NJ

DESIGN IDEAS FOR HOME STORAGE
SENIOR EDITOR: Kathie Robitz
WRITER & EDITOR: Elaine Martin Petrowski
SENIOR DESIGNER: Glee Barre
DESIGNER: Diane P. Smith-Gale
ASSISTANT EDITOR: Evan Lambert
PHOTO RESEARCHER: Robyn Poplasky
INDEXER: Schroeder Indexing Services
FRONT COVER PHOTOGRAPHY: (*top*) Jessie Walker;
  (*bottom left*) Christopher Drake/Retna.com; (*bottom center*) Eric Roth;
  (*bottom right*) Roy Inman, stylist: Susan Andrews
INSIDE FRONT COVER PHOTOGRAPHY: (*top*) Eric Roth, design: Easy Closets;
  (*bottom*) Stickley Photo•Graphic, design: KL Design
BACK COVER PHOTOGRAPHY: (*top*) courtesy of Closetmaid;
  (*bottom right*) Simon Whitmore/Retna.com; (*bottom left*) courtesy of StoreWall
INSIDE BACK COVER PHOTOGRAPHY: *(top)* melabee m miller;
  (*bottom*) melabee m miller, builder: Doyle Builders

CREATIVE HOMEOWNER
VP/PUBLISHER: Brian Toolan
VP/EDITORIAL DIRECTOR: Timothy O. Bakke
PRODUCTION MANAGER: Kimberly H. Vivas
ART DIRECTOR: David Geer
MANAGING EDITOR: Fran J. Donegan

Printed in China

Current Printing (last digit)
10 9 8 7 6 5 4 3 2 1

Design Ideas for Home Storage, First Edition
Library of Congress Control Number: 2005909005
ISBN-10: 1-58011-301-X
ISBN-13: 978-1-58011-301-4

CREATIVE HOMEOWNER®
A Division of Federal Marketing Corp.
24 Park Way
Upper Saddle River, NJ 07458
www.creativehomeowner.com

Dedication

To my father, Gerard Martin, who first said I could do anything
I set my mind to, and my mother, Elaine Martin Ferrand,
who first taught me the value of a rewrite.

Acknowledgments

With heartfelt thanks to my wonderful family
for their love, encouragement, and support;
my talented and smart colleague, Kathic Robitz, who got
me into, and out of, this project; Diane P. Smith-Gale for
her unflagging good spirits and her grace under fire;
Robyn Poplasky for her always gracious and efficient
resourcefulness; and the rest of the staff at Creative Homeowner,
who are unflappable pros and far better proofreaders than I.

Contents

ABOVE Conquer storage issues in the clothing closet with specially made racks for ties, belts, and other accessories.

RIGHT Help children learn good storage habits by providing them with easy-to-reach drawers and shelves. Keep things neat by providing some storage behind closed doors.

BELOW Stash all kinds of clutter-inducing objects, such as remote controls, magazines, and CDs, in attractive baskets and boxes.

Home storage has likely presented problems for families since man moved into the cave. If you have picked up this copy of *Design Ideas for Home Storage*, you too seek the solution to the question of where to stash all that household gear you've accumulated. Within these pages, you'll find hints on storage basics and rules of thumb for keeping things accessible. Learn how to first analyze your storage needs and then plan accessible storage for items you use on a day-to-day basis. Find valuable tips for displaying or keeping

Introduction

heirlooms safe. Discover ways to use freestanding furniture, as well as built-ins and bits of unused space, to creatively stretch the storage capabilities of your home. Learn how to organize the storage you create so that you can not only keep items but locate them quickly and effortlessly when you need them. Explore various storage solutions, and decide which products meet your needs. As you study the photographs and read the bright ideas contained here, be inspired to solve all of your storage issues once and for all.

Effective home storage means there is a designated spot for each of the hundreds of items you and your family potentially use daily. And good storage capabilities do more than keep the house neat. Well-planned storage allows you to find what you need when you want it, thereby reducing stress. Adequate storage also saves you time because you don't need to search for lost items. Finally, storage can actually save money because you won't have to buy duplicates of things you already own but can't find. This chapter includes storage ideas for all the spaces in your home that see daily use.

Day to Day

▌ start at the heart ▌ plan a pantry ▌
▌ begin and end the day ▌
▌ a place for everything ▌

For top efficiency, plan kitchen storage that includes as wide a variety of options as possible, such as open and closed shelves and both shallow and deep drawers.

Because the kitchen is the heart of the home and used by all who live there, it's a logical place to begin to work on improving storage. The first step: cull out and throw away, sell, or donate any mismatched plates and unused cookware. Group like objects, such as mixing bowls, together. Keep items that are used at the same time, such as cutting boards and knives or pots and potholders, near one another. Try to locate tools as close to their point of use as possible, which means cleaning supplies at the sink and pots and pans near the range or cooktop. Use less-accessible storage spaces to keep seasonal items, like the turkey roaster or barbecue tools. Store the most frequently used items in the storage areas that are easiest to access, generally those shelves and drawers that correspond to the space from your shoulders to your knees.

LEFT Use the storage on the perimeter of the kitchen to stash seldom-used items or things used in adjacent spaces.

OPPOSITE TOP Simple, open shelves provide storage with easy access.

OPPOSITE BOTTOM Include a sliver of space in the kitchen dedicated to cookbook storage.

bright idea

Always opt for adjustable shelves inside cabinets so you can change the positioning to meet current needs.

start at the heart

LEFT Incorporate display space in an island that separates the kitchen from other living areas.

OPPOSITE BOTTOM Reserve the open soffit for storage of collectibles or other attractive items. Because the space is difficult to reach, this storage spot is not the best place for frequently used items.

the **s**hape of **t**hings

STANDARD CABINET DIMENSIONS (in inches; size ranges increase in 3-inch increments)

Cabinet	Width	Height	Depth
Base unit	9–48	34½	24
Drawer base	15–21	34½	24
Sink base	30, 36, 48	34½	24
Blind corner base	24 (not usable)	34½	24
Corner base	36–48	34½	24
Corner carousel	33, 36, 39 (diameter)	X	X
Drop-in range base	30, 36	12–15	24
Wall unit	9–48	12–18, 24, 30	12, 13
Tall cabinet (oven, pantry, broom)	18–36	84, 90, 96	12–24

glass **a**ct

Add some sparkle to a new or existing kitchen by using glass doors on some of the upper cabinets. This not only breaks up the visual weight of a wall of cabinetry but adds character to the space. Take it a step further and use glass shelves, which permit interior cabinet lighting to illuminate the entire box. Because you can see into the cabinet, plan to finish the inside and to store decorative serving pieces or a collection there, not utility items. (If you must store things like food or appliances in these particular cabinets, choose opaque or textured glass so that the contents are obscured.) For safety's sake, don't use glass doors on base cabinets. If you do, invest in tempered glass, especially if you live with children.

LEFT A simple jug can hold cooking implements at the ready.

keep it together

OPPOSITE TOP LEFT Tools and ingredients necessary for baking should be stored together in a cook's kitchen.

OPPOSITE TOP RIGHT Dividers in drawers keep contents from becoming a jumble.

OPPOSITE BOTTOM Items such as bakeware, cutting boards, and serving trays are neatly and efficiently stored between vertical dividers.

set up a system

Inside the fridge (or pantry), store items in the same place all the time and you won't need to spend time hunting for the mayonnaise or tracking down the eggs. Make it a habit, for example, to keep condiments on the door; milk cartons and beverages on the top left; butter and cheese in the keeper; and leftovers on the bottom shelf. In the pantry, group recipe staples on one shelf, cereals on another, and snacks elsewhere. You'll not only save time but easily keep tabs on items that are running out. Encourage all family members to maintain the system.

keep it at hand

dish **up**

For everyday dishes, here are several appealing approaches
to storage:

▌**Stack them in large, deep drawers.** Line the bottom of the
drawers with pegboard, and use movable pegs to corral plates and
bowls in neat stacks.

▌**Display them.** Plate racks, on their own or integrated into a bank
of cabinetry, put your dishware on display while keeping it handy.

▌**Use a built-in drying rack.** If you intend to use a built-in plate
rack for drying your dishes, make sure it's installed where the wet
dishes can drip into the sink.

▌**Organize cupboard interiors.** Should you choose to keep dishes
in a cupboard, check out the array of minishelves that allow you to
separately stack plates of different diameters so that you can easily
get access to them one at a time.

OPPOSITE TOP LEFT
Keep everyday glasses near
the drinking water source.
▌
OPPOSITE TOP RIGHT
Retrofit a hinged bin into an
existing kitchen sink front
panel for sponges and
cleaning gear.
▌
OPPOSITE BOTTOM LEFT
Spices can reside on a pullout
near the range.
▌
OPPOSITE BOTTOM RIGHT
Store pots on heavy-duty
rollouts right under the
cooktop.

keep it on view ||||||||||||||||

bright idea

personality

It's convenient—and often attractive—to keep some frequently used items on hooks, racks, and shelves. The secret to doing this successfully is to be sure that the items stored on display are those that are either rotated or used and replaced regularly so that they stay clean and don't become dust catchers.

OPPOSITE TOP LEFT A small decorative shelf keeps mugs right on hand but still out of harm's way.

OPPOSITE TOP RIGHT Display cooking and measuring gadgets with spices at the range.

OPPOSITE BOTTOM Keep dinnerware and serving pieces close to food preparation areas.

LEFT Stash everyday dishes in a plate rack above the sink.

BELOW House cookware and cookbooks within reach of the range.

An efficient pantry is the ultimate in kitchen storage. A well-planned pantry provides a place to keep staples and backup supplies. However, one size pantry does not fit all. To plan a pantry that works for your family, first look at the types of foods you regularly buy. It makes no sense to plan a pantry that holds stacks of canned food if you don't

plan a pantry

buy food in cans. Similarly, don't include a spice rack for dozens of small spice bottles if yours is a salt-and-pepper crowd. Measure the packages of the items you do buy for a clue to shelf placement. Again, adjustable shelves are a smart choice because of the flexibility they offer. Ideal pantry depth is between 18 and 24 inches. Any deeper, and you won't be able to reach the packages stored at the back of the shelves. And while rollout shelves add to the cost, they are a must for deep pantries because you can bring shelf contents forward without having to move items.

LEFT Convert a reach-in closet to an efficient pantry with readily available components, including adjustable shelving; solid, woven, or wire baskets; vertical dividers; racks; and so forth.

LEFT Take an inventory of what you plan to store. Reserve the prime eye-level storage space for items used most often.

BELOW LEFT The contents of this narrow but deep pantry are easily reached because all the shelves pull forward.

BELOW RIGHT Plan to store light items on the doors of the pantry and heavy items on interior shelves. Sturdy wire racks allow for ventilation but may permit small packages to fall through.

begin and end the day

Because of both space constraints and the daily activity level, the average family bathroom presents many storage challenges. In most homes, this is the room where every inch of potential storage space must be used. If you are remodeling, take advantage of any design services offered. Even if there is an extra charge, the return on investment can be well worth it. In an existing bath, you'll need to be more creative. Cull medications and cosmetics, and discard those you no longer use. Corral the remainders in clearly labeled, see-though plastic bins. Use a spice rack to store toiletries inside the medicine cabinet. Keep cleaning supplies together in a clear plastic bin stashed under the vanity or on a high shelf of the linen closet if you live with little ones. Put the space on the back of the door to good use by adding a towel rod or robe hooks. Label shelves throughout the space so that all family members can help maintain the storage system.

OPPOSITE A tall storage cabinet makes good use of wall space that might typically be wasted. Add dividers, bins, or baskets to drawers so that smaller items don't end up in a jumble. Assign each family member his or her own drawer.

RIGHT Handsome storage cabinets in close proximity to the sink or vanity keep grooming supplies and toiletries on hand but out of sight.

bright idea

magnification

Even a moderate expanse of mirror helps a small space appear larger while doubling the available light.

cabinets in the **b**ath

The design attention that has been focused on the bathroom for the last several decades now has improved every aspect of the space. The vanity still reigns as the major supplier of storage in the bath, but these days it looks better, stores more, and has grown taller. Because one height does not suit all people, stock vanities now range from the standard 30 inches to 36 inches high. With two vanities in the master bath, each one can be tailored to a comfortable height for its user. Vanities are also available in several depths. The 18-inch-deep units free up floor space while 24-inch-deep models store more. To improve the bathroom storage picture even more, manufacturers continue to add the option for additional cabinets, open shelves, and freestanding furniture. Even the humble medicine cabinet has increased in size, functionality, and good looks.

ABOVE There's plenty of space for towels, cosmetics, toiletries, and cleaning supplies in this triple vanity configuration.

RIGHT Maximize storage potential. Flank a single sink with two tall storage units.

vanity and **c**abinet **d**imensions

STOCK BATHROOM CABINET DIMENSIONS (based on standard sizes in inches)

Cabinet	Width	Height	Depth
Sink base	15-72	28-36	16-21
Drawer base	12–21	31½-34½	21-24
Tall linen cabinet	9-24	83-96	21
Vanity linen cabinet	9-18	48-83	21
Vanity hamper cabinet	15-18	31½-33½	21

RIGHT Avoid visual clutter. Keep most toiletries behind closed doors, and use open shelves for decorative items and neatly folded and stacked towels.

storage and the pedestal lav

Pedestal lavatories are one of the most popular options in today's bathrooms for good reason. Available in many decorative styles and sizes, their classic proportions are elegant and timeless, and their lithe shapes and dainty footprints make even the smallest bath feel larger. But when it comes to storage space, pedestal lavs provide none. Be creative about adding your own. One option: purchase a separate piece of furniture that provides some storage nearby (below). Or install a recessed tall cabinet into the wall nearby to save space in a small bath (center). Flank the lav with drawer bases, and top them with a durable work surface such as granite, tile, or laminate (opposite). Another option: seek out a large and deep medicine cabinet that can take up some storage slack. If none of these ideas appeals to you, use the pedestal lav in the powder room, where storage needs are usually minimal.

bright idea

coordination

To help unify a bath space, choose storage components from one manufacturer's line, and use the same finish on all hardware and trim.

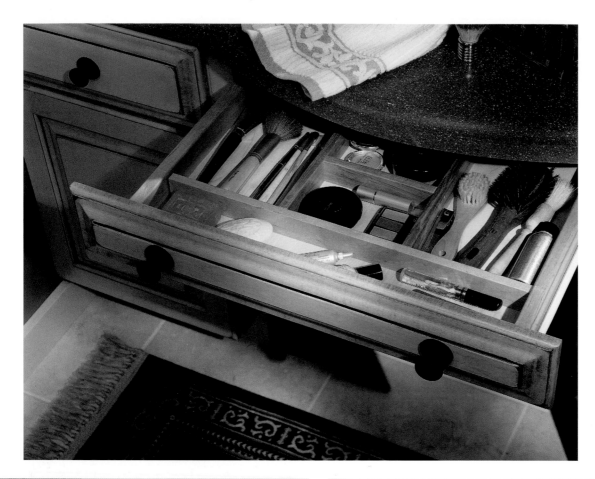

LEFT Divide and conquer bathroom clutter with ready-made drawer inserts in wood, plastic, metal, or wire mesh.

BELOW LEFT You'll find a wide array of shelves, bins, and racks designed to fit on the inside of cabinet doors that can be adapted to stretch storage capabilities in the bathroom.

BELOW RIGHT A sturdy rolling cart adds movable storage to the bath.

choosing a medicine cabinet

You can find attractive medicine cabinets that can be wall-mounted or recessed into a nonload-bearing wall between the studs. From ultra-contemporary versions in glass and metal to designs that make bold architectural statements, there's a wide selection of stock units to match any decor or cabinet style.

When shopping for a medicine cabinet, look for one that offers room for everything from toothbrushes to shaving cream and bandages. Choose one that spans the width of your vanity or beyond it, if wall space allows. In other words, buy the largest one you can find! Look for deep shelves that accommodate

objects larger than a small pill bottle. Built-in lighting, swing-out mirrors, and three-way mirrored doors are some of the other extras you may want in a medicine cabinet. In addition, some units come with a lock or a separate compartment that can be locked to keep potentially dangerous substances out of the hands of young children.

Be sure to carefully read the storage recommendations on any prescription medications, vitamins, and herbal supplements you plan to store in the medicine cabinet. Many do not fare well in the high humidity of the bath and are best kept elsewhere.

details add storage potential

recess space

One way to stretch the storage capacity of the bath—or any other small room—is to create recessed niches in the spaces between the studs inside the walls. Located near the vanity, niches like those shown below provide a convenient spot to stow a few extra towels or grooming supplies. Or specify that a recessed niche be incorporated into the wall of the shower area to keep soaps, shampoos, and shaving creams at the ready. Locate another niche near the toilet to hold an extra roll or two of tissue. Easy to maintain and waterproof, ceramic tile that can be wiped clean is one of the best finishing options for the inside of niches in the bathroom.

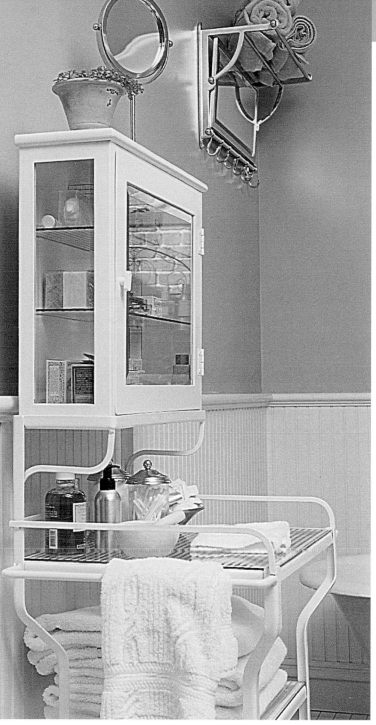

details add more function ▮▮▮▮▮

ABOVE Look for an attractive, freestanding cabinet to hold grooming supplies and other bath accessories. Be certain the finish is durable enough to stand up to the moisture that's often generated in the bathroom.

TOP RIGHT Free up floor space and keep dirty laundry corralled with bins or baskets set in deep drawers.

RIGHT Improve efficiency in the bathroom, where there are dozens of small items to store, by adding a shelf inside a cabinet. To improve function more, choose a sturdy rollout that brings contents forward to the user.

a place for everything

Bedrooms, whether for children or adults, present yet another unique set of daily storage challenges. Built-ins that surround the bed, under-bed storage boxes and drawers, and nightstands or bedside tables that incorporate some drawers or shelves will all help to maintain order and produce the desired sense of serenity. When it comes to kids, they not only sleep and dress in their bedrooms, but also store books, toys, and games and need some space for play. In addition, children's rooms must continue to evolve as they grow. So it's especially important to choose flexible pieces. For example, a timelessly designed, sturdy, adjustable bookshelf that holds stuffed animals for the toddler and puzzles and toys for the child will continue to be useful for books and other media for the 'tween or teen.

bright idea
accessibility

Kid-friendly storage must be accessible to them. Stackable open bins and see-through boxes on adjustable shelves make it easier for kids to put their things away.

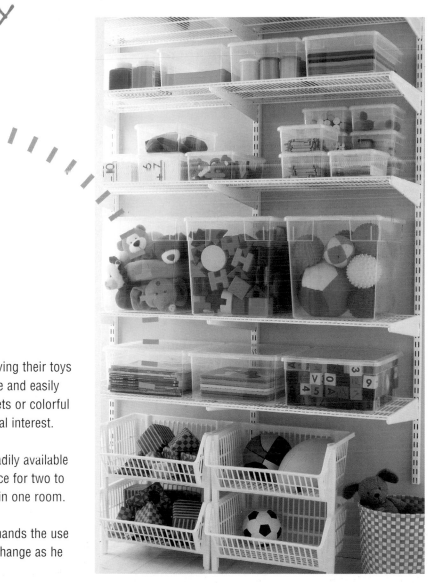

OPPOSITE TOP LEFT Children enjoy having their toys stored out in the open where they can see and easily find them. Use identical lightweight baskets or colorful bins to stash toys and provide some visual interest.

OPPOSITE TOP RIGHT Loft beds are readily available in many styles and provide sufficient space for two to share sleeping, storage, and study areas in one room.

OPPOSITE BOTTOM A child's room demands the use of flexible storage components that can change as he or she grows.

storage equals serenity

ABOVE Turn an unused section of bedroom wall into storage with a handsome armoire or cabinetry. They are available in many sizes to complement every decor.

LEFT Shelves built in to a headboard turn the bedroom into a book lover's haven. Add good lighting and a tabletop surface for comfortable reading in bed.

OPPOSITE Stow extra bedding in a bureau or blanket chest located at the foot of the bed. Move a small chest of drawers next to the bed to do double duty as a commodious nightstand.

Closed cabinets hide extra supplies and help to keep the laundry room tidy.

Plan to include some space to hang no-iron garments as they emerge from the dryer. This space is also useful to drip dry items.

Assign each family member his or her own laundry bin or basket. Fold and sort clean items into the appropriate basket as they come out of the dryer.

If space allows, include a sink for soaking stained items and hand-washing sweaters and delicates.

laundry ideas

Here are several tips for maximizing storage:

▌ **A stackable washer and dryer** can fit into a closet, hall, or bath.

▌ **Install a shelf above side-by-side laundry** gear to hold supplies.

▌ **Store bleach pens, stain removers, and lint rollers** in a bin or basket on the shelf.

▌ **Toss all the loose change** that accumulates in an unbreakable jar, or stash unmatched socks in a bin or basket until their mates appear.

▌ **Keep a small sewing box** with a needle and a variety of threads to fix loose buttons and snaps before they are lost.

▌ **Install a pullout wire basket** in the laundry room cabinetry to hold those last few items waiting for tomorrow's first wash.

Store a fold-down ironing board and iron behind a door. It makes quick touch-ups easy.

2

The most aesthetic form of storage, display space lets you attractively organize items so that they are out of the way yet always visible. Well-planned displays allow you to keep treasured items safe while adding personality to a space. There are many ways to integrate decor with organization throughout the home. Plan a wall filled with framed photos or art. Fill a tabletop or shelf with a pleasing arrangement of pottery. Or house a collection of china in glass-fronted kitchen cabinetry or on a dining room plate rail. This chapter provides ideas for attractive and useful display storage.

On Display

▮ storage as decor ▮ in the right light ▮
▮ adaptive reuse ▮

Some display storage is strictly for decorative purposes. Other items, such as this brightly painted collection of pottery, are utilitarian and meant to be used on a frequent basis.

LEFT A display of earth-tone pottery pieces perfectly suits the natural theme of a sleek brick, wood, and stone dining space.

BELOW LEFT A collection of vintage lunch boxes occupies custom-built cubbies installed above the cabinetry in this bright and whimsical kitchen.

OPPOSITE A glass-fronted cabinet prominently displays the blue china pieces that provide the accent color for this fresh and inviting dining room.

Decorative objects, such as pottery, baskets, china, toys, or a collection of unique or colorful items, present almost limitless possibilities to add visual impact and expressive character to a space. Keep in mind that a collection has greater visual weight when it's presented as a cohesive whole rather than dispersed individually around the room or throughout the home. To ensure that your treasures are a genuine decorative asset, rather than just too much clutter,

storage as decor

always group like items together in a manner that emphasizes their shared traits, such as all the blue-and-white pottery on one shelf of the cabinet, all the green glassware on another. Sorting and displaying decorative items by color, size, material, or subject matter calls attention to them. For even greater decorative impact, display collections that relate to the architectural style of your home, such as sleek, high-glazed pottery in a modern space or chunky Arts and Crafts pieces in a simple Craftsman bungalow.

RIGHT Apple-green walls and crisp white-painted shelves are the ideal background to showcase a collection of blue-and-white china in a charming family gathering space.

BELOW A display of eclectic and unusual early-model home appliances shows how to group items by type for the greatest visual impact.

OPPOSITE TOP Antique brown-and-white china pieces complement a farmhouse-style kitchen.

OPPOSITE BOTTOM Colorful vintage pottery, displayed on a plate rail, enhances the architectural style of an Arts and Crafts dining room.

displays set the decorative tone of a space

bright idea

play it up

To make items visually
"pop," consider painting
the inside of a cabinet
or the wall behind the
shelf a color that
contrasts sharply
with the items
on display.

bright idea
visibility

See-through glass
or plastic containers
allow close monitoring
of the contents,
ensuring timely
refilling.

ABOVE LEFT Built-in niches and nooks
in the bathroom provide handy storage
for a few extra towels or a tube of hand
cream.

ABOVE RIGHT Staples stored in identical
screw-top glass jars are both attractive
and functional.

LEFT A focal-point painted cabinet
displays decorative serving pieces at
the ready in a busy kitchen.

OPPOSITE Everyday dinnerware stored
on open shelves and plate racks adds a
zip of color to a neutral space.

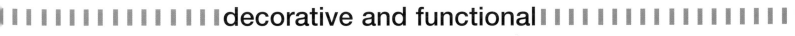

decorative and functional

types of **s**helving

Decorative shelves come in so many varieties that they are best categorized by their basic construction:

▎**Bracketed Shelf.** Bracketed shelves are the most common type—a flat shelf surface supported by right-angle brackets. Brackets of all descriptions can be bought at home centers and hardware and woodworking stores, and ornately decorated versions are available through millwork companies. Bracketed shelves are often built as one piece, with or without a back panel between or behind the brackets. When one-piece units have no back panel, a mounting cleat installed along the back shelf edge makes for easy installation.

▎**Plate-Rail Shelves.** A plate rail is typically considered a trim detail but is in essence a decorative shelf. With a narrow shelf usually supported by brackets or crown or cove molding, a plate-rail shelf is used for displaying plates, framed pictures, and such. It has a groove cut into its top surface for holding the edges of plates.

▎**Cleated Shelves.** Cleated shelves are supported on the sides and back by one-by cleats secured to the wall. They are often used for storage shelves in closets but work well as decorative shelves if the cleats aren't too noticeable. They are a good option for rounded corner shelves.

▎**Suspended Shelves.** Suspended shelves hang from cables, chains, or all-thread (threaded rods) and have a distinctly contemporary look. They can hang freely from the ceiling or be supported by angled lengths of cable or chain secured to the wall.

▎**Cantilevered Shelves.** Cantilevered shelves have no visible supports, thus appearing to defy gravity. In reality, the shelf surface may be secured to the wall framing or installed as shown at far right. Installing cantilevered shelves is more complicated than installing other types, but the result is an exceptionally streamlined appearance with an artistic built-in quality.

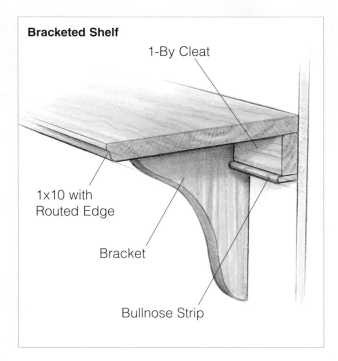

Bracketed Shelf

1-By Cleat

1x10 with Routed Edge

Bracket

Bullnose Strip

Cleated Shelves

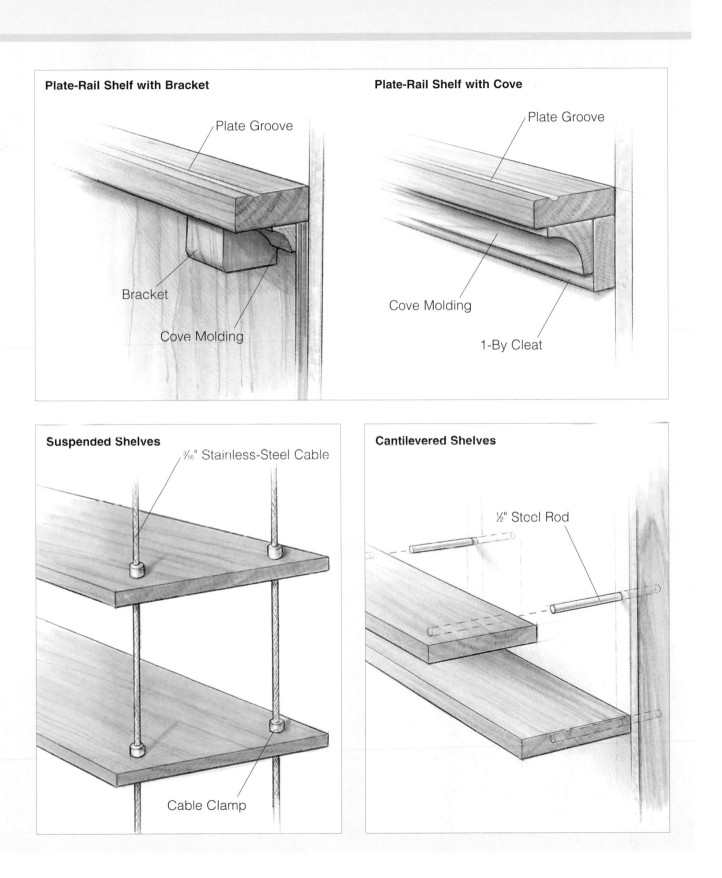

Plate-Rail Shelf with Bracket

Plate Groove

Bracket

Cove Molding

Plate-Rail Shelf with Cove

Plate Groove

Cove Molding

1-By Cleat

Suspended Shelves

3/16" Stainless-Steel Cable

Cable Clamp

Cantilevered Shelves

1/2" Steel Rod

bright idea

glue it

Adhere smaller decorative objects to shelves with a tiny dab of removable clay-like adhesive, found in most craft stores. This way, the pitchers stay put on the shelf when the kids chase each other down the hall.

display dos and don'ts

There are no hard and fast rules about what will or won't work as a display object. However, there are guidelines to determine how to display what you select.

▌**Group objects by similarities.** Choose items that share the same color, material, shape, or motif.

▌**Vary the elevation.** Include elements of differing sizes and heights.

▌**Add depth.** Don't always place objects in a straight line, which can look static. Instead, stagger pieces from front to back, or put some on an angle.

▌**Don't overdo it.** If there are too many items on display, they look like clutter. Store extra items out of sight, and freshen up your display with those pieces every so often.

OPPOSITE TOP Select several decorative moldings that suit the style of your home, and install them high on the wall to keep a collection of fragile objects on view but out of harm's way.

LEFT Support glass shelves with a series of handsome decorative brackets.

BELOW A simple molding, painted and installed at chair-rail height, provides accessible shelving for a child's toys.

There is no one "right way" to hang a collection of art. Try arranging paper templates of the pieces until you find a layout that pleases you.

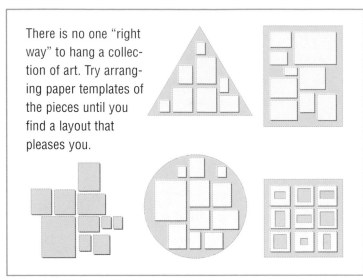

|||||||||||||| arranging is an art ||||||||||||||||||||||||||||||||||||

ABOVE Use similar simple black gallery-style frames to pull disparate pieces into a cohesive display.

BELOW Antique wooden farm tools make a strong statement when grouped together and contrasted against a white wall.

ABOVE A collection of brightly colored antique game boards becomes a decorative asset when hung as a grouping in a stairwell.

create a series

Small- or medium-size artworks are more impressive when placed together on a wall. If you are displaying drawings or photography, make sure that the frame is large enough to accommodate a mat. For an up-to-date look, make the mat at least 6 inches larger than the photograph or illustration. This is an effective way to draw attention to a small piece of art. Rather than choose a mat color from the surrounding room, instead pull it out of the work of art. That way the mat will always work with the piece, no matter where it hangs.

LEFT Frame similar pieces identically, and then hang them in a tight grouping. As a general rule, art should sit 6 to 9 inches above a sofa or chair or at eye level when you are seated.

Casting your collections in the best light is an intrinsic part of an effective display. Contemplate how you want your displays to be perceived: do you want to accent one special piece or several? A spotlight, positioned at a 30-degree angle to your display, is the answer. If you prefer a more ambient wash of light to show off your collection or you'd rather emphasize texture, transparency, or some other nuance in the artwork, pay a visit to a reputable showroom and meet with an accredited lighting designer.

in the right light

ABOVE Ensure that colorful, decorative pieces such as these are easy to see by installing light fixtures inside glass-fronted cabinets.

RIGHT Glass shelving allows light from above to illuminate the items stored on the lowest shelves.

OPPOSITE A combination of lighting types, including wall washers and low-voltage cabinet lights, capitalize on the books, art, and collectibles that add personal warmth to this contemporary space.

illuminating facts

▎**Track Lights.** The versatility of track lighting makes it appealing to people who change their wall displays on a regular basis. Track systems are surface mounted, so installation is typically less involved than hard-wiring a new circuit. They come in both standard line and low voltages and are sold in 3- to 4-foot lengths; connectors are available that allow the installation to expand as needed. Fixtures can be found in an enormous range of decorative styles, ranging from vividly colored Murano glass shades to miniature stage lights.

▎**Recessed Lights.** Another popular method of illuminating wall art or a collection is with recessed downlights, often called canister lights. These lights are set flush with the ceiling so there is no visible light fixture or bulb—a definite plus for rooms with clean architectural lines. Canister lights may be fitted with many accessories, such as baffles, apertures, and shields that let you control the angle, diffusion, and spread of light beams.

▎**Strip Lights.** For collections that sit on shelves or in niches, small strip lights installed at the front edge of a shelf or concealed behind some trim along its sides can provide a pleasing, evenly lit appearance. Properly locating the light fixtures is important. Through experimentation you may find that backlighting is more effective than downlighting your curios.

I f you don't seem to have just the right shelf or cabinet for displaying a favorite collection, don't let that stop you. Look around your home, in resale shops, or at flea markets for objects you can adapt for display storage. The possibilities for creative recycling are limitless.

adaptive reuse

Keep in mind: when it comes to collectibles, sometimes less really is more. Because you can't possibly display every copper pot or decoy ever made, be selective in what you display. And if you find that you already have far too many of one collectible to show off all at the same time, sell or give some away and rotate the remaining pieces seasonally.

LEFT A wooden blanket stand holds a collection of vintage handwoven baskets.

BELOW An heirloom plant stand provides a sturdy home for a pottery collection.

LEFT Leave the doors open on a painted corner cabinet, and it becomes a display case.

BELOW The varied heights of the rungs on a vintage wooden ladder create an effective way to show off every decoy to its best advantage.

boxes

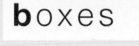

A grouping of decorative boxes that suits the style of your home can fill a multitude of storage gaps.

When neatly stacked on display, boxes bring color, texture, and personality to a room while providing a way to conceal all kinds of objects—CDs and craft, sewing, or office supplies, to name just a few—that might otherwise add to visual clutter. You'll find a wide variety of suitably sturdy boxes readily available at office supply and home decorating retail stores and in catalogs. For a cohesive look, keep all the boxes in the same space the same color or material. And look for boxes that incorporate attractive labels so you can catalog the contents for easy access.

found objects

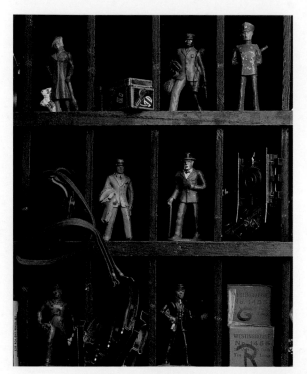

Scour flea markets and resale shops for vintage divided boxes, such as those used for tools and packing or printer's type. Use them to showcase many related small objects in one spot. This treatment eliminates the visual clutter often associated with displaying small things. The objects gain instant importance, and the display becomes a decorative asset.

bright idea
try again
Don't hesitate to try many different arrangements of decorative objects until you find one that pleases you.

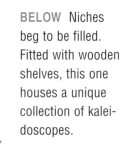

BELOW Niches beg to be filled. Fitted with wooden shelves, this one houses a unique collection of kaleidoscopes.

LEFT An unused fireplace becomes display space.

BELOW A dress dummy sports the favorite jewelry of the lady of the house. A fabric-covered dummy might hold pins as well.

add wit and whimsy ||||||||||||

3

Both practical and attractive, built-in features, such as nooks, niches, bookcases, and shelving, can add more to your home than convenient storage. Properly executed built-ins are useful design elements that often add architectural interest where none existed. They can imbue a room with character and a sense of craftsmanship, or unify your home by making the most of sloped ceilings, half walls, and irregular spaces. Look for opportunities to add built-ins—for example, to define an opening, separate rooms, or fill odd spaces beside a fireplace or under a stairway.

Built-ins

I many options I increased function I
I architectural detail I
I oddly shaped spaces I

Trimmed simply and painted white, these open bookshelves unify the space, add storage and display capabilities, and lend some character to the room.

many options

Built-ins range from simple, open niches tucked into an odd space to an entire room filled with elaborately trimmed bookcases. The style of your home and your budget will determine how detailed the built-ins are. The most expensive units are custom-made and finished by a cabinetmaker, who painstakingly plans and measures them to fit the exact dimensions of the available space. More affordable built-ins are sometimes fashioned from ready-made, unpainted shelving and bookcase components that are attached to the wall, trimmed with moldings that suit your home, and then painted in place. Still others are constructed with prefinished stock kitchen cabinetry components. (See "Building Window Seats," pages 78–79.)

ABOVE LEFT At a standard depth of 15 in., wall-cabinet components, such as these contemporary, warm, wood-toned built-ins, provide ample floor-to-ceiling storage without intruding on the available floor space.

LEFT A simply executed, built-in bookcase balances with the farmhouse style of this room.

bright idea

strategize

Before you add built-ins, inventory what you plan to store in them so you can decide on open or closed shelves, or a combination of both.

BELOW Trimmed with decorative moldings and painted to complement the focal-point fireplace and mantel, these traditionally styled built-ins contribute much to the architectural interest of the space.

Well-planned built-ins can add function throughout the home. Consider built-in cubbies and a bench in the foyer or mudroom to hold outdoor clothing and gear. In the family, living, and dining rooms, plan built-ins with closed compartments to stash toys, games, serving pieces, and so forth, out of sight. Include some open shelves for displaying the family's favorite decorative objects and books. Free up some floor space in the bedroom and bath by including partially recessed

increased function

built-ins in those spaces. Or perhaps consider a built-in headboard that includes open and closed storage and some lighting or a platform bed with built-in drawers. Nooks and niches in hallways, entries, on a stairway landing, or in a passageway can provide a striking way to add interest and to display decorative items. Make use of the sometimes oddly shaped spaces under the roofline, where standard furniture pieces might not fit, to add built-in drawers or bookcases. Consider how built-ins might improve a hallway or divide a large space into two cozier ones while providing storage.

OPPOSITE Turn a passageway into a bar or butler's pantry by adding standard cabinetry components.

LEFT An inviting bead-board banquette tucked into the kitchen provides dining space and a spot to display family treasures.

ABOVE Double the function of your home office by adding a built-in bed that includes sleeping and storage space for overnight guests.

bright idea

maximize

Extend custom-made, built-in bookcases all the way to the ceiling. Use the higher shelves for out-of-the-way display space, or add doors to the top shelves and stash infrequently used items there.

LEFT Plan open shelves for the electronic components that require air circulation, and then add some closed storage in drawers or behind doors where you can keep compact discs, DVDs, instruction booklets, and warranties.

ABOVE Use built-ins to capitalize on a charming fireplace and to provide a home for the television in a traditionally styled living room.

OPPOSITE TOP Floor-to-ceiling towers and a bridge that spans the width of the bed add many linear feet of hidden and display storage without taking up much floor space in this bedroom.

OPPOSITE BOTTOM Add architectural detail and provide a place for books and games with simple, but elegant, bookcases.

built-ins do double duty

IIIIIIIIIIIIIIIIIIIII add storage to every room IIIIIIIIIIIIIIIIIIIIIII

TOP A custom-designed built-in wall unit is the sturdy base for a home aquarium. It also includes handsome concealed storage for fish-tank accessories, supplies, and fish food.

ABOVE Drawers tucked under the bed provide unobtrusive storage in a bedroom where the view is the focal point.

think it through

Unless you have sufficient hands-on carpentry experience to do it yourself, installing built-in storage can be an expensive proposition, so plan carefully before you begin. To get started:

▌**Keep a file** of ideas clipped from books and magazines. Note the similarities in the built-ins that appeal to you.

▌**Pay attention to** the scale of built-ins in relation to the room. Will the bookcases you're considering take up too much space in the hallway? Is the window seat too small for the landing?

▌**Pick an appropriate style.** Elaborate moldings and carved corbels may appeal to you, but do they really suit the architectural style of your home?

▌**Choose materials wisely.** Painted units can be refreshed easily. Stained natural wood built-ins add warmth and elegance, but they can darken a room and appear imposing.

RIGHT Bring more function to the dining room with display space in glass-fronted wall cabinets with hidden storage in the base units. The counter-top functions as a buffet server.

BELOW A French Country hutch houses the television, conceals utilitarian serving pieces, and provides display space for collectibles in the dining area of this kitchen.

map it out

Not sure there is sufficient space for the built-ins you're dreaming about for your home? There is an easy way to find out. First, decide on the preliminary measurements for the units. Then make a template of the proposed pieces using sheets of newspaper or outlined in masking tape on the floor. Live with the outline for a few days to be sure traffic flow and furniture placement are not adversely effected.

use built-ins to

OPPOSITE A desk and tall shelving separate this home office space from the mudroom.

BELOW TOP Divide large expanses of open space with utilitarian built-ins. This unit houses electronic gear and provides a cubby for holding firewood. Note that the divider is low enough to allow light from the large windows in one room to spill into the other.

BELOW BOTTOM Spacious cookbook storage is built into the back side of one wall of an open-plan kitchen.

divide larger spaces

ABOVE Painted bookcases separate the living space from the foyer, but still allow a view to the front door.

create serene and snug private places

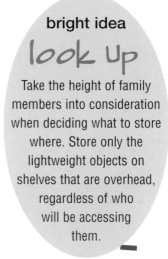

bright idea

look up

Take the height of family members into consideration when deciding what to store where. Store only the lightweight objects on shelves that are overhead, regardless of who will be accessing them.

ABOVE LEFT A tall wardrobe and nightstand offer convenient storage in the bedroom.

LEFT A floor-to-ceiling unit incorporates numerous drawers and doors, thereby eliminating the need for additional furniture in a traditionally styled bedroom.

sweet dreams, super storage

A custom-built bed that incorporates storage can make the most of the tiniest bedroom for your smallest family members. As these playfully designed examples illustrate, it's possible to tuck a platform bed into a corner (left) or to plan a bed to include a sloping ceiling (below right) as part of its charm. For the most efficient use of limited space, include a sturdy platform bed that incorporates two side-by-side drawers installed underneath for clothing or extra bedding. If storage needs demand more, it is possible to stack two or three drawers below the bed platform. But keep in mind that this raises the level of the platform so that it becomes necessary to provide portable steps (below left) or a ladder so little ones have safe and comfortable access to the bed. Add a bookcase or two to hold favorite reading materials, toys, and personal treasures. And for comfortable bedtime reading or studying, be sure to incorporate adequate lighting controlled by a nearby switch.

architectural

interest

No matter what the architectural style of your home, it's always possible to add built-ins to suit. Moreover, if the interior of your home is that of a bland-box tract house, adding built-ins provides the perfect opportunity to bring in some interesting detailing along with all-important storage. Keep in mind that the size and scale of built-ins should be appropriate for the room. For example, small rooms, or those with ceilings that are 8 feet tall or less, will have a harder time supporting a heavily detailed, built-in hutch than a larger room with 10-foot ceilings. Similarly, if you plan to add built-ins to more than one room, coordinate the various elements from room to room to bring a sense of balance and unity to the spaces. For example, if you plan white-painted bookcases with a bead-board back panel for one room, consider the same or a similar treatment for built-ins in an adjoining space. Or if you add fluted moldings to trim a built-in server in the dining room, use the same trim in the kitchen and butler's panty.

OPPOSITE TOP LEFT A basic room becomes an inviting personal library when floor-to-ceiling shelves surround a doorway or window.

OPPOSITE TOP RIGHT Customize built-ins to suit what you want to display or store. This unit includes an open area that's ideal for displaying colorful art.

OPPOSITE BOTTOM These painted bookcases flank an entertainment center that includes additional storage concealed behind doors.

ABOVE An elegant arched niche sets the decorative tone of a formal room.

fixed or **a**djustable?

Adjustable or fixed is the eternal shelf question. The pros and cons for each are straightforward: you can move adjustable shelves, but their means of adjustment (standards, clips, pins) can detract from the appearance of a built-in. Fixed shelves stay where you put them but offer a somewhat more finished, formal, "built-in" appearance. One possible compromise: install the adjustable shelves behind doors and use fixed shelves for areas that will remain open and on view.

LEFT Grand-scale built-ins suit a soaring space while filling many functions. These include both display and hidden storage and a desk area, and can work as buffet servers.

set the decorative tone

LEFT A sleek and contemporary display and storage unit suits this open-plan home.

LEFT Bead-board built-ins with glass doors above offer display area in a country-style great room.

ABOVE Niches for displaying art, sturdy but minimalist bookshelves, and base-cabinet units combine to create an orderly and personalized home office.

BELOW Arches and traditional trim lend a formal look to the storage cupboards in this dining room.

bright idea

practical

Keep a footstool or stepladder in close proximity to tall units so that you can reach the objects on higher shelves for cleaning.

a cozy retreat may incorporate storage

ABOVE The two tall book-cases flanking this window seat help to create the appearance of a nook. The bridge above visually lowers the ceiling height, making the seat feel cozy. A thick cushion and throw pillows add comfortable seating.

LEFT A large staircase landing is the ideal spot for a cozy window seat. This one includes several drawers for spare blankets.

window seat details

The size and height of the sitting surface are critical to the comfort of a window seat. Pay attention to these measurements when doing your planning:

▌ **Seat depth.** The depth of the seat from the front edge to the window should be a minimum of 22 inches, with the same width for the back support. Any additional depth will make the seat more comfortable to use. Angled sides add comfort for sitting or, if there isn't sufficient space, you can compensate with plump pillows. If the seat will be used for napping, plan on a depth of 30 to 36 inches.

▌ **Seat width.** To plan the width of the seat, take into account everyone who while use it and for what purpose. A minimum width for an average-sized person seated parallel with the window is about 36 inches. Seats intended for napping or overnight sleeping must be at least as wide as the tallest sleeper's height, plus several inches more to accommodate blankets and pillows. For architectural balance, a window seat should be at least 8 to 12 inches wider than the window. This allows room for trim work or other decoration without crowding the window.

▌ **Seat height.** A good starting seat height is 15 inches above the floor. The addition of a medium-to-firm foam cushion at least 3 inches thick will put the seat height even with a standard chair or bench. A few inches of variation either way will not be problem. However, keep in mind that taller seats can be less inviting, and that lower seats will feel uncomfortably close to the floor.

building **w**indow **s**eats

The best cabinets to use for a window seat are the short wall units designed for installation over a refrigerator. At 15 inches tall and 24 inches deep, these cabinets are good building blocks for using as is, or as a base that will have a few inches added here or there as needed. If your window seat will go into an existing alcove, the cabinets should fit fairly well, but you can always hide gaps at the sides using filler boards. Home centers carry stock cabinets (the cheapest option), or you can order semicustom cabinets (more expensive but with better selection) from a cabinet showroom. In either case, try to match the cabinet door styles and finishes to any other cabinetry in the room.

❙ **Build the frame.** Following the basic installation shown here, start with a 2x4 base built to match the width of the alcove, and fasten it to the floor and wall so that the base is perfectly level and its front edge is flush with the cabinet face-frame. For a taller seat, use 2x6 lumber for the base. Center the cabinet over the base, and secure it with screws driven into the wall and base. If there are

Window Seat Made with Standard Over-the-Refrigerator Cabinets

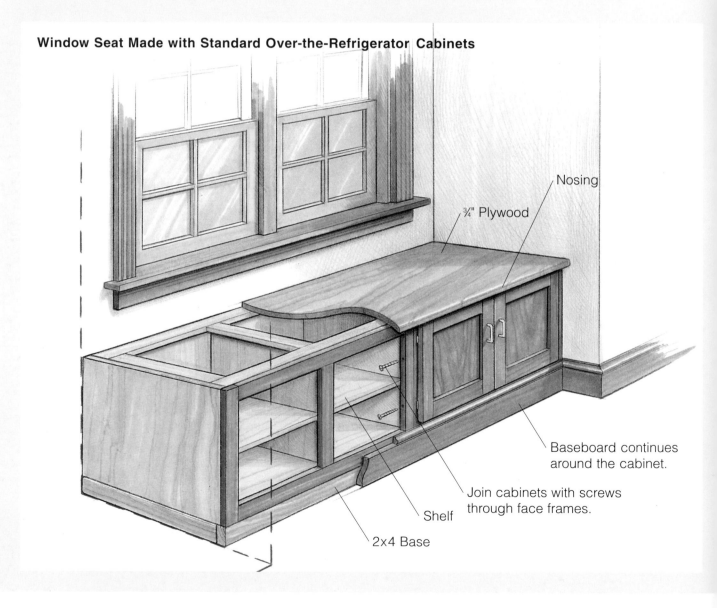

Nosing

¾" Plywood

Baseboard continues around the cabinet.

Join cabinets with screws through face frames.

Shelf

2x4 Base

multiple cabinets, screw them together through the face frames before installing. If necessary, cut filler boards from material that matches the cabinets and install them by screwing through the face frames. To create an alcove, use pantry kitchen cabinets to flank the window seat as shown below.

Cut the seat. Make a seat from ¾-inch plywood that has a veneer that matches the cabinet, or use MDF if you plan to paint the seat. The seat should fit tight to all of the walls. Finish the front edge of the seat with nosing trim or iron-on veneer tape. Secure the seat to the top cabinet edges using construction adhesive.

Add final touches. Finish by adding baseboard and other trim to hide the window seat base, and apply caulk or small trim to cover any large gaps along the seat or filler boards.

Window Seat Made with Kitchen Pantry Cabinets

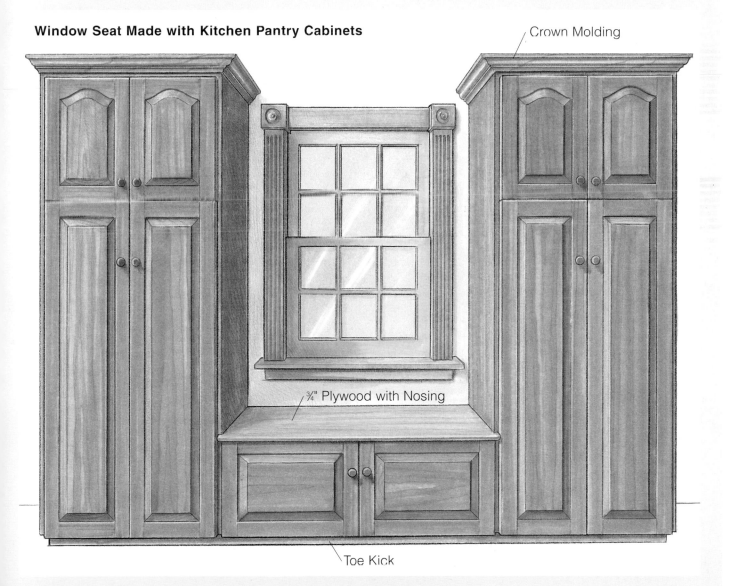

Crown Molding

¾" Plywood with Nosing

Toe Kick

good seats

A good cushion makes all the difference for a window seat. For comfort and durability, choose a cushion with a medium-to-firm foam core covered with cotton batting. Most cushions start at about 3 inches in thickness. The quality of the fabric you choose for the cover is also important. For durability, select upholstery grade material. In kitchens or other areas where the cushion is likely to be easily soiled, apply a stain-resistant treatment, or choose a machine-washable fabric. The cushion fabric should be fade-resistant if the seat will get much direct sunlight. A zipper at the back makes the cover easy to remove for washing.

bright idea

illuminate

Planning a window seat as a cozy spot to curl up with a good book? Be sure to include adequate lighting installed where you can reach the switch.

OPPOSITE TOP Assemble stock cabinetry components to fill a wall with useful storage and an inviting window seat.

OPPOSITE BOTTOM Drawer bases incorporated into a window seat near the entry provide ideal storage for items such as hats, gloves, and scarves.

ABOVE A window seat that includes open shelves for books becomes a favorite family reading spot.

RIGHT A banquette in the dining area incorporates storage for infrequently used or awkward oversized items, such as vases, large bowls, baskets, or platters.

oddly shaped spaces

Unusually shaped spaces, or those with oddly angled walls or ceiling, are often great locations for built-ins because they allow for clever use of an otherwise wasted, under-utilized, or unadorned area. Oddly shaped spaces may require some custom construction, but it's often possible to start with a square or rectangular modular unit, such as a low bookcase, and then add elements to fit the space. Some likely but unusually shaped spots to consider for adding built-ins include under a staircase, in a dormer or under the eaves of the attic, in the recesses beside a fireplace, under or between two windows, flanking or surrounding a doorway, or in a wide hallway or passage.

OPPOSITE TOP A cleverly designed wall of built-ins adds storage, seating, and character to a family living space.

OPPOSITE BOTTOM A gable can be put to good use as an inviting window seat. Even the knee wall has become useful with built-in seating.

ABOVE Built-ins that follow the line of the staircase add architectural interest and provide both open and closed storage as well as display space.

LEFT An odd nook gains purpose by adding a built-in desk flanked with tall display space.

make the most of nooks and crannies

BELOW Add simple bookcases and wide ledges to the spaces in between windows.

RIGHT Open shelves turn unused wall space adjacent to the doorway into an inviting spot to curl up and read.

evaluate need

Before you buy or construct any built-ins, ask yourself the following questions:

❙ What will I store there?

❙ How sturdy must the shelves be?

❙ Will I include display space?

❙ Will I include storage for items best kept behind closed doors?

❙ Will adjustable shelves add more function?

❙ Will I need to add lighting to make the built-ins functional?

RIGHT A dining room hutch includes drawers for table linens as well as display space for a colorful collection of china.

▮

BELOW The glass doors on this functional, shallow pantry that's tucked into a hallway make finding items easy.

▮

BELOW RIGHT A banquette dining area is made more useful by adding an overhead shelf for decorative objects and a convenient bookcase to stash cookbooks nearby.

build a **b**asic **b**ookcase

The case shown here is made with ¾-inch plywood with a ½-inch plywood back panel and a face-frame made of one-by hardwood boards. The shelves are attached with screws driven through the side pieces. Wood plugs hide the screw heads. If you want to install multiple units, add plugs to only the exposed sides of the end units.

❚ Assembly. To build the bookcase, cut the side pieces ½ inch wider than the shelf depth to create a recess for the back panel. Cut the shelves and top piece to size (shelves over 32 inches wide will require mid-supports). If desired, add nosing trim or veneer tape to hide the front edges of the shelves. Assemble the carcase with coarse-thread drywall screws driven through counterbored pilot holes. Cut the back panel; make sure the carcase is square; then attach the panel with glue and brads. Also nail through the back panel into the shelves. You can install 1x2 mounting cleats underneath the bottom shelf and above the top shelf for more strength.

❚ Installation. Install the case by screwing through the mounting cleats and into the wall framing. Install the face-frame with glue and finishing nails. You can preassemble the frame using biscuits or install it one piece at a time. Add molding or one-by trim boards along the top and, if desired, along the bottom of the case. Match any existing base molding to create a built-in look.

Bookcase Construction

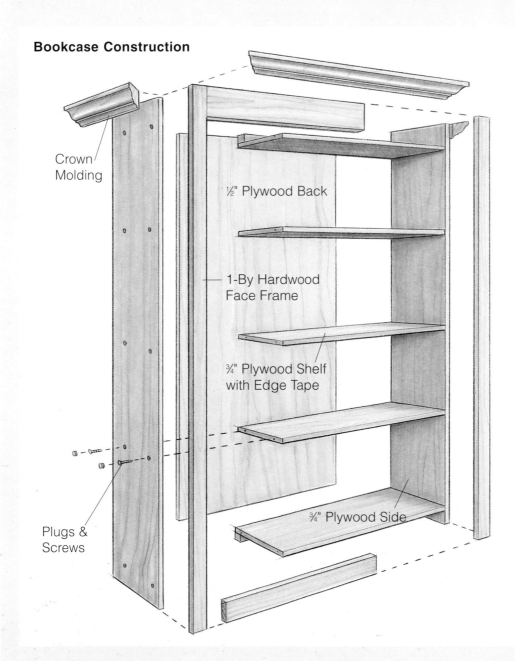

Crown Molding

½" Plywood Back

1-By Hardwood Face Frame

¾" Plywood Shelf with Edge Tape

¾" Plywood Side

Plugs & Screws

make **m**odular **u**nits **l**ook **b**uilt-in

There are several tricks to fool the eye of even a careful observer. Molding is the best tool of deception because it hides gaps around modular shelving units and ties multiple units together into a seamless whole. Trim can also be used to decorate the built-in to match details elsewhere in the house. For example, if a room has baseboard or crown molding, wrapping the same molding around an added bookcase will make it look like it was installed by the original builder. The illusion is most effective if the style of the built-in complements or blends with the character of the house. A rustic, knotty-pine cupboard won't look like an original part of a contemporary interior, just as a white melamine bookcase will stand out in any historical setting.

Recessing a unit (right top) is another way of making an add-on look built-in. Even a partial recess will help. If you can't cut into a wall to recess a unit, you can fur out the wall around the bookcase—that is, add a second wall layer of 2x4 studs (or even 2x2s) and drywall to build up the wall's thickness after the unit is installed. Another option that works for units that rise to within 18 inches of the ceiling is to build a soffit (right below) to fill the space between the unit and the ceiling, similar to the treatment applied above kitchen cabinets. The soffit can run straight up from the unit or be L-shaped, with the lower (horizontal) part of the L meeting the unit at a right angle. The latter design creates a box that can house recessed light fixtures that illuminate the front of the built-in.

Choose a wood type or painted finish that matches other room elements. And you can further enhance the built-in look by adding unit doors styled after interior room doors. Built-in doors that include glass can be modeled after the home's windows. When units are completely recessed and trimmed, consider using the same casing that appears on windows and doors.

ABOVE Fit an efficient home office with plenty of concealed storage into a sliver of space.

ABOVE RIGHT Recessed shelves provide attractive display storage without taking up any floor space.

RIGHT Make the most of oddly angled walls by adding built-ins, such as the multifunction cabinets and shelves tucked into this home office.

OPPOSITE TOP Handsome built-ins follow the curve of this family room wall.

OPPOSITE BOTTOM The odd angles of a sloping ceiling become an asset with the addition of an open bookcase.

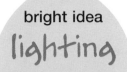

bright idea

lighting

Adequate lighting will make reading book titles and finding items in the cabinets below easier.

Freestanding furniture is yet another way to add attractive storage throughout the home—provided you choose pieces that are functional as well as beautiful. The type of furniture you select will depend on your style, space, and budget, as well as what you plan to store. For example, bookcases and entertainment centers suit the needs of living and family rooms especially well. A desk that includes file drawers can turn any room into an efficient home office. In addition, even the bed provides storage if you choose one with head- or foot-board compartments and under-the-bed drawers.

Movable Pieces

I casegoods I containers I

It's possible to find stylish furniture pieces, including shelves, chests, tables, and armoires, that will solve storage problems in every room of your home.

BELOW One advantage of freestanding furniture, such as this tall piece that includes display and hidden storage, is that it can be moved from room to room as needs change.

RIGHT This bedroom is not only pretty but smart, too, because it incorporates plenty of concealed storage provided by a nightstand with drawers, a small chest at the foot of the bed for extra linens, and an armoire.

OPPOSITE This stylish room includes storage for a mattress in the trundle bed. Bookcases offer open and closed storage, adjustable shelves, and a drawer.

Storage furniture is available to suit a wide range of needs. In the furniture industry, it is referred to as casegoods because of its box-like structure (although tables also come under this category). It may include bookcases or any other type of open shelves, cabinets with hinged or sliding doors, cabinets that house audio or video equipment, breakfronts, chests, armoires, or desks. Casegoods come in many shapes and

casegoods

sizes and offer a place to display or protect collectibles and other valuables. Modular pieces can be used to create storage walls or room dividers. Storage walls are connected units that fit from floor to ceiling. They divide space while providing access to storage from both sides. Room dividers serve a similar purpose but do not extend to the ceiling or from wall to wall. They are most commonly used to divide living and dining areas.

the basics

The term **"casegoods"** refers to any piece of furniture that is used for storage, such as a chest of drawers; tables are also part of this category. The furniture industry uses a variety of labels to denote the construction materials used. The meanings of these labeling terms are regulated by the Federal Trade Commission.

▮ **Solid wood** ("solid oak" or "solid pine," for example) means that the exposed surfaces are made of solid wood without any veneer or plywood. Other woods, such as plywood, may be used on unexposed surfaces such as drawer sides and backs.

▮ **Genuine wood** means that all exposed parts of the furniture are constructed of a veneer of a type of wood over hardwood plywood.

▮ **Wood** means all of the parts of the furniture are made of some type of wood.

▮ **Man-made materials** refers to plastic-laminate panels. The furniture may also include molded plastic that mimics wood panels, carving, or trim.

bright idea

measure

Make a scale drawing of the room you're furnishing, including the location of permanent fixtures, such as doorways and windows. Take it with you when you shop to be sure the items you're considering fit the space.

find a perfect storage fit

quality checks

When shopping for wood furniture you'll find varying levels of quality and pricing. Use this checklist to judge what you're getting for your money.

Frames
❙ Veneers and laminates should be securely joined to the base material.
❙ Joints bearing weight should be reinforced with corner blocks.
❙ Back panels should be screwed into the frame.
❙ Long shelves should have center supports.

Drawers
❙ Drawers should fit well, glide easily, and have stops.
❙ Drawer bottoms should be held by grooves, not staples or nails.
❙ Drawer interiors should be smooth and sealed.
❙ Drawer corners should have dovetail joints.

Doors
❙ Cabinet doors should open and close smoothly.
❙ Hinges and other hardware should be strong and secure.

Finishes
❙ All finishes should feel smooth unless they are intentionally distressed or crackled.

OPPOSITE Select freestanding pieces, like this pyramid-shaped display case, that fit the spaces you have.

ABOVE LEFT For the most flexibility, choose furniture that includes both open and closed storage.

LEFT Whether you shop for something new or recycle an existing piece, look for furniture that suits your style and your storage needs.

ABOVE Putting an antique (or a clever reproduction) to good use as display space is an attractive way to boost storage in any room of the home.

storage and the foyer or mudroom

Try to integrate the furnishings of the front entry with the tenor of your interior. This can be done without compromising the storage in the space. Recycle a small chest of drawers (below) to hold cold weather gear in the foyer of a country home. If the space just inside the front door is tiny, a shallow console table (opposite top) makes an attractive resting place for handbags and briefcases while coats are being shed. If you're a collector of antiques, an ornate coat rack (opposite bottom left) with a built-in hinged-top bench fulfills several storage needs simultaneously. The entry of a country-themed or traditional home might feature a rustic wooden bench (opposite bottom right) that doubles as a table and seating. If it suits your climate, an umbrella stand is a thoughtful (not to mention pragmatic) touch that will save your floors from puddles while containing the unwieldy accessories. For the modernist with a bit more space, a stainless steel framed mirror that pivots to reveal a shelf and several hangers makes a design statement as well as provides storage. Should a stairway run down to your entry foyer, and if the design of the surrounding spaces permits it, the triangular cavity of space beneath the stairs can present an opportunity to increase your storage capacity significantly. A cabinetmaker or skilled carpenter can craft a combination of closets, drawers, or shelves to fit the area. These built-ins can service the entryway or any of the adjacent rooms, holding anything from clothes to books to bottles of wine.

IIIII for every room of the home IIIIIIIIIIIIIIIIIIIIIIIIIIIIIIIIIIIIII

ABOVE Store an entire home office in one tall piece of furniture. Workstations such as this one are available in many styles, and they typically can house computer equipment and office supplies.
I
OPPOSITE TOP One way to maximize storage in the living or family room is to choose tables that include drawers, which are ideal for stashing the remote control or the newspaper out of sight.
I
OPPOSITE BOTTOM Make sure kids can reach the storage area of tall pieces used in their rooms. For safety's sake, bolt tall pieces directly to the wall studs.

be picky

When it comes to selecting furniture pieces that will also provide ample storage, it pays to be a bit choosy. Before you buy, carefully compare and analyze your top choices. Choose freestanding furniture pieces for utility, not just good looks. Ask yourself

❙ **Does the amount of storage** a piece offers justify giving up the floor space it will occupy?

❙ **Are shelves deep enough** to hold what you plan to store on them?

❙ **Are shelves sturdy enough** to hold the weight of what you plan to store?

❙ **Can you add to or modify** the piece to meet your needs? For example, consider adding vertical dividers, bins, or stacking boxes to make the best use of space inside furniture.

advantages of furniture

There are some advantages to planning at least some storage in movable pieces of furniture, such as new or antique armoires, nightstands, and chests. Movable pieces are more flexible than built-ins because they allow you to

▌ **Add storage pieces** as needs change.

▌ **Modify the interior** of pieces to suit current needs.

▌ **Move furniture** from room to room as storage needs change.

▌ **Take your storage** with you if you move.

bright idea

what's in it?

The decision to choose between furniture with cabinets or drawer storage should hinge on what you plan to store.

ABOVE The desk surface of this secretary folds up to hide the office when it's not in use. The deep bottom drawer holds either legal- or letter-size files.

LEFT Some furniture, like this buffet chest, offers the flexibility of both door and drawer storage.

BELOW LEFT Maximize function by choosing pieces that offer more than one form of storage space. This unit does triple duty as a nightstand and bookcase that offers the bonus of concealed storage in the drawers.

BELOW One advantage of freestanding book or display shelves is that you can move them if storage needs change.

fill storage gaps with furniture

BELOW Instead of a tabletop, choose nightstands that incorporate drawers or closed cabinet storage.

OPPOSITE BOTTOM RIGHT This composite table is designed to be covered with a decorative cloth that extends to the floor so that objects stored on the shelves are not visible.

OPPOSITE LEFT Even a graceful demilune table can provide a shelf and some drawer storage for a hallway, bedroom, or other small space.

OPPOSITE TOP RIGHT In the family or living room, use furniture that offers some storage as a side table, such as this replica watchmaker's cabinet. It provides five drawers and includes a pullout work surface that could easily hold a beverage or book.

variations on a theme

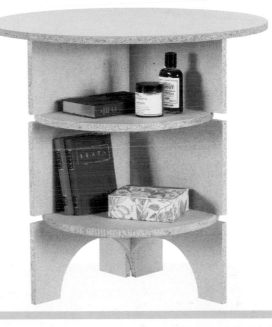

keep it up

All storage systems in every room of the home require periodic maintenance to keep them functioning optimally. Here are some tips to keep your storage system in good shape.

❚ **Make it a habit** to immediately discard broken objects that cannot be repaired.

❚ **Give or throw away duplicates** unless you use them regularly.

❚ **Discard all the miscellaneous items you are keeping** "just in case." It's usually wiser to free up the storage space to use on a daily basis.

earthquake-aware storage

If you live in an area of the country that is susceptible to earthquakes, you'll need to take some extra precautions when planning storage.

▌ **Secure tall and top-heavy pieces**, such as bookcases, shelving, and armoires, to the wall with braces or strapping. Be sure braces are attached to wall studs.

▌ **Put heavy objects** in the bottom cabinets, near the floor, not on the top shelves.

▌ **Use museum putty** or hook-and-loop fasteners to adhere objects to shelves.

▌ **Bolt or tether electronic gear** and other heavy objects directly to shelves that are secured to the wall studs.

▌ **Check that cabinet doors** throughout the house latch securely. A magnetic catch will not stand up to an earthquake. Try childproof latches instead.

▌ **In the garage** and other utility areas, fasten cabinets with hooks and eyes or spring-loaded catches.

▌ **Store breakable treasures**, such as great grandmother's heirloom china, with foam pads between pieces.

▌ **When packing breakable items** in boxes for long-term storage, fill all gaps with crumpled or shredded paper, bubble wrap, or packing peanuts.

OPPOSITE LEFT
You'll find free-standing specialty furniture, such as this handsome corner media center, that is designed to solve specific problems.

OPPOSITE RIGHT
A tall, slim cabinet can maximize storage in a small room, such as the bathroom or guest bedroom, where it could hold stacks of extra towels or linens. A mirrored door offers extra function and may make the space appear larger.

TOP LEFT
Choose a dining room console with tempered glass doors if you own attractive serving pieces to display. If not, select a console or buffet with solid doors so you can stash things unseen.

LEFT It's possible to conceal a bar or beverage center within a classically detailed armoire.

bright idea
flexibility

One or two deep drawers offer more storage flexibility than many shallow drawers do.

I how to paint furniture

SIMPLE HAND PAINTING

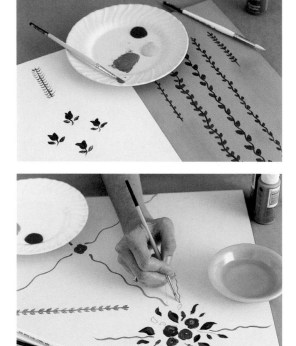

You will need: Acrylic paint in various colors I Fine artist's brushes, including flat, liner, pointed, and round in assorted sizes I Pencil I Sponge I Paper towels I Transfer paper

The most important advice about hand painting is to use high-quality artist's brushes. Cheap ones lose bristles and leave brush marks. Always practice on a board or paper before painting on the real surface (top right). Begin by marking the placement for the design and drawing it lightly with a pencil. Or you can use transfer paper to trace patterns that you can carry over to the surface or object you are decorating. Position the traced motif in place on your project, and slip a piece of transfer paper between the motif and the project. Retrace the lines of the motif, using a ballpoint pen to transfer it onto your project. Using an artist's flat or round paintbrush and the colors of your choice, dip the brush into the paint, and then dab off a bit of the paint. Gently guide the brush, allowing it to do the work, pressing down and easing up to vary the thickness of the line (bottom right). Always keep a damp sponge and paper towels handy for quick cleanup. If you make a mistake, wipe off the paint quickly and try again.

HAND PAINTING FROM A STENCIL

You will need: Assorted acrylic paint colors I Stencil brushes I Stencils I Ballpoint pen I Spray adhesive I Fine artist's brushes: 1-inch flat, medium liner, medium round, #2 or #3 pointed I Paper towels I Chalk pencils I Ruler or straightedge

Paint the object or surface in any desired finish coat, and allow it to dry. Position the stencil on the surface to be decorated using spray adhesive to hold it in place. For extra support, tape it down. Using a pencil, trace the outlines of the stencil's shapes (top right). Once you've traced the entire design, remove the stencil template. Even though you will not paint the design entirely freehand, it's a good idea to practice on a board. This way, you can make brush strokes and create shading with confidence later. Using artist's flat and round paintbrushes and the colors of your choice, fill in the outlined areas of the motif (bottom right). Double- or triple-load a flat paintbrush with different colors to add dimension. Use a stencil brush and a small amount of paint to create texture or a blush of color.

ABOVE Recycle an old armoire, or buy a new unpainted piece, and turn it into an attractive and practical family heirloom with a simple paint technique.

bright idea
ambiance

Decorative baskets or boxes can add storage as well as character and personality to a space.

E very organized home should include plenty of small-scale storage. That's where portable containers, such as boxes, bins, and baskets, which are readily available in all shapes, sizes, materials, and colors, come into play. Whether made of wicker, wood, wire, metal, plastic, cardboard, or a combination, these types of storage devices are essential in keeping household clutter under control. For example, simple open baskets corral items yet offer accessibility, and they're great for bath supplies, kitchen utensils, socks, underwear, and accessories. Use attractive boxes on shelves, in closets and cabinets, and even on display. Maximizing the function of any closed storage container requires labeling. Also, keep in mind that the containers you buy for storage must themselves be stored somewhere and that they will be more difficult to use effectively if they are stacked atop each other. Finally, don't choose a container that is so large that it's impossible to lift when full.

containers

OPPOSITE Repurposed antiques do double duty, providing both storage and display.

LEFT Woven baskets are not only attractive but allow air to circulate; so they are ideal for storing food items, such as root vegetables, in a cool, dark place.

BELOW Choose boxes or baskets with lids so that items that are not used every day stay clean and dust-free.

ABOVE LEFT In the moist environment of the bath, corral odds and ends in open and airy containers, such as wicker, rattan, or wire baskets, which will allow air to circulate.

LEFT Colorful, easily accessible baskets make short work of cleanup for kids.

ABOVE Use a clever step basket to hold those items that always seem to accumulate while awaiting transport to a different level of the home.

OPPOSITE TOP It's always a smart idea to label the outside of storage containers so that you know what's inside without having to open them.

OPPOSITE BOTTOM Fabric-covered boxes are attractive enough to leave out in the open. They make ideal storage for personal items, craft and hobby supplies, or CDs and DVDs, for example.

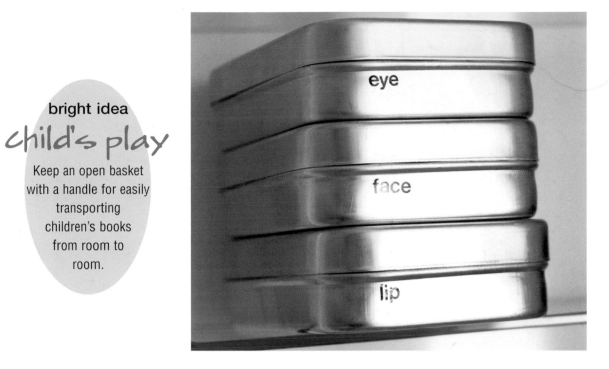

bright idea

child's play

Keep an open basket with a handle for easily transporting children's books from room to room.

put boxes, bins, and baskets to work

| | | | | seek opportunity | | | | | | | | | | | | | | | | | | | | | | | | | | | | |

BELOW Small children will be more likely to keep their rooms orderly if storage is geared to them, so keep it open and accessible.

OPPOSITE TOP Attractive boxes can do double duty as end tables. Just be sure they are sturdy.

OPPOSITE BOTTOM Look for furniture pieces that can do more than one job at a time. These ottomans also incorporate storage and could be invaluable in a home office or family room.

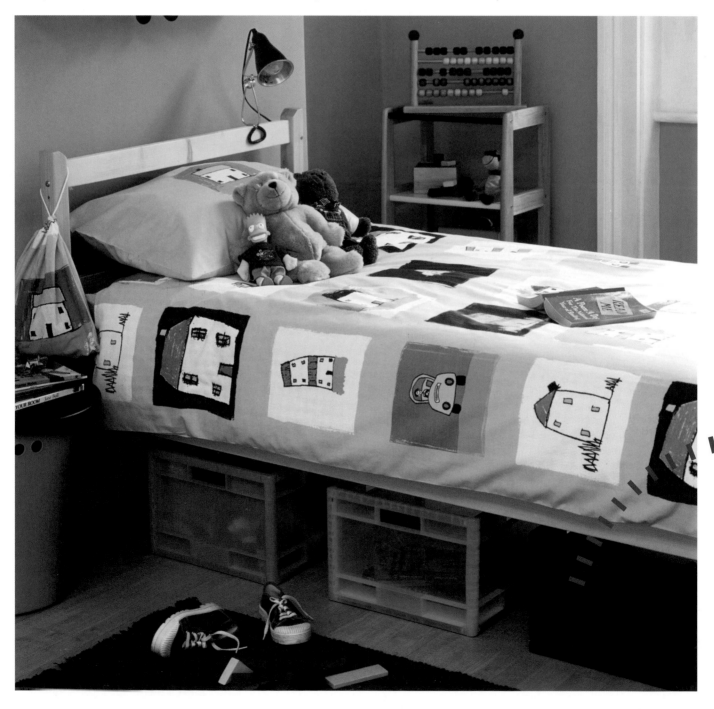

rules of **t**humb

When it comes to finding spots to incorporate storage into your home, don't pass up any opportunity. If a piece of furniture is to take up valuable floor space, make sure it earns its keep by providing at least some storage capacity. And if you live in an apartment or a smaller home, make it your mission to find furnishings that help alleviate any storage crunch you might be feeling.

▌ **Organize storage** in a neat and logical way. Keep objects near where they are used: for example, games in the family room. If usage habits change, move the object.

▌ **Keep the items** you use the most in the most prominent and easily reached spaces.

▌ **Label boxes and bins** on the side of the container that is visible once it is stored. Use indelible, waterproof markers in an easily readable color.

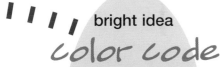

bright idea

color code

Color code portable storage for kids' things either by child —red is Andrew's, yellow is Kate's— or by function, such as blue for toys, green for clothing.

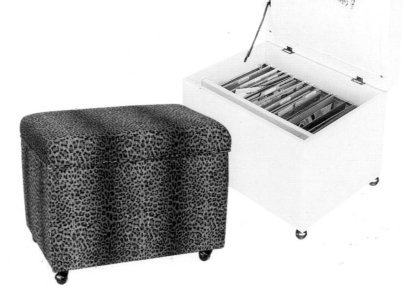

The backbone of storage in most homes is the closet. And while the ideal might be a huge walk-in closet, the reality is that if your home is more than a few decades old you need to find ways to stretch the space in much smaller closets. When it comes to maximizing closets, today's homeowners are in luck. Home centers and storage retailers make it easy to find components designed to make the most of existing closets by using racks, dividers, double-hanging bars, cubbies, drawers, and more. This chapter provides inspiration and offers ideas you can adapt to make the most of your closets.

Closets

**▌ his, hers, and ours ▌ walk-in closets ▌
▌ kids' closets ▌ linen closets ▌
▌ design it yourself ▌**

A well-organized closet includes a variety of storage options to accommodate hanging and folded garments, as well as shoes and other accessories.

The bedroom closet holds a substantial part of everyone's wardrobe, and in all likelihood a good deal more. Even if your closet is in critical condition—it's virtually impossible to slide hangers easily along the rod, for example—there are ways to improve its usefulness without breaking the bank, or your back.

You can double or even triple the closet's hanging space by installing additional rods lower in the closet to suspend clothes such as skirts, blouses, shirts, jackets, folded trousers, and other shorter items. Don't enter into this undertaking without the proper preparation. Especially if you've never planned a fitted closet before, guesstimating is not good enough. Once you have thoroughly culled your wardrobe, categorize, count, and measure the length of the garments you'll be storing. To determine the position of the rods, you need to know both the linear feet, as well as the hanging lengths, of your complete wardrobe.

his, hers, and ours

A full-service closet needs to provide more than well-orchestrated hanging space. Shoes, bags, sweaters, and accessories need to be stowed, too. Once again, take an unflinching inventory of these items and measure the keepers. When you're ready to devise your closet's configuration, you have a choice: take the measurements to an organizational consultant (whose services are often included in the price of closet systems purchased from home-storage retailers), or head to your home workshop.

OPPOSITE TOP LEFT The height of the pole in a closet is not arbitrary, but rather is determined by the length of the garments that will be stored there.

OPPOSITE TOP RIGHT It's always wise to include a full-length mirror in the closet or on the back of the door.

OPPOSITE BOTTOM LEFT Try to limit the height of any stacks of folded clothing to no more than three or four garments, or they will tumble over when you try to remove one from the middle.

OPPOSITE BOTTOM RIGHT Choose drawers that fully extend so that you can easily view all the contents at one time.

ABOVE To keep clothing at its pressed best, avoid overcrowding hangers.

| | | | | | | | | organize shared space by using stackable shelves,

does your closet measure up?

To help you plan an optimally functioning clothes closet, here are the standard lengths (in inches, measured from the pole) for hanging everyday garments. If you are taller than average, be sure to raise the pole a bit higher so that garments won't graze the floor.

Men's Clothing		Women's Clothing	
Pants, folded	32	Bathrobe	52
Pants, unfolded	48	Blouse	36
Shirt	38	Dress	58
Suit	40	Evening gown	69
Ties, folded	32	Skirt	35
Topcoat	56	Suit	37
Winter coat	55	Winter coat	52

individual cubbies, and other closet accessories ||||||||||||

OPPOSITE LEFT Measure the length of your clothing before you shop for closet-stretching components. Count shoes and pocketbooks as well so that you plan sufficient storage.

OPPOSITE TOP RIGHT Soft padded or plastic hangers are less likely to leave marks on clothing.

OPPOSITE BOTTOM RIGHT Bring a pair of shoes with you when you shop to be sure they fit in the storage devices available.

ABOVE LEFT An adjustable lattice features attached pegs and is a relatively inexpensive way to organize accessories at your fingertips, one key to making your closet work for your wardrobe.

ABOVE RIGHT Set aside part of the closet for double-hanging shirts and pants.

RIGHT Don't overlook the inside of the doors when maximizing the interior of a closet.

bright idea

easy access

A folding or—better yet—collapsible stool that can be stored in the closet will make it easy to access items on shelves.

LEFT If you can't stash a step ladder in each closet, keep one on each level of the home.

BELOW It's important to select drawers in a variety of widths and depths to accommodate different types and sizes of clothing.

OPPOSITE TOP These dividers attach to the shelf and help to keep folded stacks of clothing tidy.

closet-**s**tretchers

Shelves for folded garments can run the full height of the closet, or if you don't require that much flat storage, place them at about chest height for optimal accessibility. Shoes and boots can go in cubbies or see-through plastic boxes near the floor. Angling the bottom shelf can give you a better view of its contents. Or look for specially designed racks or fabric pockets to hold several pairs of shoes. Hats and purses, bagged or boxed against dust and scuffs, find a home in the upper shelves of the closet.

LEFT You'll find pullouts that hold belts, scarves, and ties.

ABOVE A larger walk-in closet affords space for a roomy hamper. This wire model attaches to the inside of a hinged door and allows air to circulate around the clothing.

walk-in closets

ABOVE Custom-built closet components take the place of bedroom furniture and create the ultimate walk-in closet.

ABOVE RIGHT Outfit shallow drawers with inserts for jewelry.

A walk-in closet should measure at least 5 x 7 feet. This will allow room for storage along two walls and still leave enough of a path into the space to survey its complete contents. Unlike a dressing room, where clothing is concealed and protected behind closed doors, everything hanging in a walk-in closet is visible at one time, making the design very efficient. Walk-in closets, like reach-in styles, can be fitted out with tiered hanging rods, drawers and cubbies, shelves, racks, and trays to put every last inch of space to work.

A dressing room should be lined with reach-in closets, cabinets, and casegoods of varying dimensions. A table or central island can hold grooming supplies or act as additional storage. For comfort's sake, you'll want a minimum of 50 square feet of space to accommodate the various forms of storage in the space, while allowing for clearance to walk around and change clothes without being hemmed in. You might be able to find this kind of space in a large master bedroom along an outside wall—which would also provide the opportunity to incorporate the requisite window or two into the dressing room.

RIGHT Provide flexible clothing storage by including as many varied storage forms as possible.

BELOW Compartmentalizing items as much as possible allows you to see and find things at a glance.

BELOW RIGHT If you can include a bench, the walk-in closet becomes a comfortable dressing area.

ABOVE LEFT Colorful shoe pockets could also hold hats and mittens, hair ornaments, and the like.

ABOVE RIGHT Most kids have too many toys to play with at one time. Store some in sturdy boxes on the top shelf of the closet, and periodically rotate toys in and out of use.

RIGHT A folding laundry bin is one tool that might help kids keep their rooms neat.

OPPOSITE LEFT Choose shallow drawers as opposed to deep ones for kids so that they can easily locate items.

OPPOSITE TOP Infants' clothing is small enough to triple hang. Later, turn the space at the bottom of the closet over to toy storage or a laundry basket.

OPPOSITE BOTTOM Choose adjustable poles and shelves that you can move as your child grows.

The most important guiding principle for planning a child's closet is to put things where he can reach them. Because the easier the closet is for the child to use, the sooner he'll be able to take care of his belongings. Always choose an adjustable shelf system for a child's closet so that you can easily change the height. Plan to store out-of-season gear on the upper shelves,

kids' closets

and use the floor and the side return spaces for toys and shoes. Buy sturdy, correctly sized hangers, and limit the height of stacks of shirts to just two or three garments. While hooks are easy for kids to use, avoid hanging sharp ones at eye-level. And do provide a convenient drop-off point, such as a plastic or wicker basket, on the floor of the closet for dirty laundry.

RIGHT If space allows, the dining room or kitchen is an ideal location for a closet where you can store pressed table linens on hangers or dowels.

OPPOSITE TOP To conserve space, use bypass or slide-by doors or screens on a linen closet in a small bathroom or narrow hallway.

OPPOSITE BOTTOM It's possible to use stock cabinetry to create a customized linen closet that resembles fine furniture.

linen closets

Because the hallway linen closet is generally used by everyone in the family, you may need to take some extra measures to keep it organized and thus maximize its function. Label the shelves in the linen closet—"twin sheets" or "bath towels," for example—so that everyone who uses it knows exactly where each item belongs. If you stack towels and sheets with the fold facing the front of the linen closet, these items are easier to grab. The closet looks neater, too. Keep complete sets of bedding together—pillowcases folded around both top and bottom sheets—to quicken the process of changing the sheets. When not in use, comforters and duvets (cleaned, folded neatly, and bagged with a cedar sachet) should occupy the topmost shelves of the linen closet, leaving everyday linens and towels to the shelves that are within easy reach.

closet doors

Believe it or not, the kind of door on a reach-in closet can have an impact on the quantity and quality of your storage. A standard hinged door can act like an auxiliary wall surface; both its front and back sides can be fitted with hooks or hanging pouches or pockets that can be stuffed with socks, scarves, and other small accessories. A hinged door poses one drawback for small bedrooms: its outward swing eats into the open space in the room. If that's an issue for you, consider installing either a bifold door or an accordion-style design. Both of these configurations permit the complete contents of the closet to be fully exposed, but the doors—because of their opening mechanism and relatively small surface area—do not lend themselves to being the basis for supplemental storage as a hinged door does. A set of bypass or sliding doors also solves the swing-space problem, but these can only be installed as a set of two or more, making them suitable for closets with openings that are wider than 3 feet. A pair of side-hinged doors can also be employed in this situation.

bright idea

stand-in

Don't have the space
for a full-fledged linen
closet? Look for a
tall piece of furniture
that you can use as
a linen press.

ABOVE Provide hanging space for both long and short items, and sufficient light inside the closet to allow you to see colors correctly.

RIGHT Slide-by doors do save space in the room, but also conceal part of the closet interior when opened.

OPPOSITE LEFT A large walk-in closet can easily accommodate a bank of drawers. The countertop surface above this unit provides a handy spot for matching accessories or stacking clean laundry waiting to be stored.

OPPOSITE RIGHT Count the long and short items you plan to store and measure the width of folded items so that you can plan sufficient shelf space. Be aware that bulky extra-large sweaters require more shelf width than do small T-shirts.

Apropos of the bedroom, dream. What do you need—and wish—to get out of your closet storage? Nearly every scheme includes purely pragmatic hanging space, but now's the time to fantasize. Would life be perfect if you could see every pocketbook in your collection all at once? Would dedicated sock drawers send you (or your spouse) to nirvana? Maybe you've always wanted to shelve your sweaters in the closet rather than the dresser.

Go through magazines, catalogs, and books, and tear out or copy photos of closets that inspire you. Take notes on what you like about each installation; then make a master list of amenities. Consider appearances: do dark woods appeal, or light-colored, low-maintenance laminates? Should the closet

design it yourself

doors be hinged or sliding? Solid or louvered? Do you like basket-type drawers or are you partial to the conventional box style? Then think about the functional features that have caught your attention. From dressing tables and full-length mirrors, specialized racks for shoe storage, segmented trays for rolled ties, and more—the list of closet-storage options and add-ons is a long one.

With your vision of a perfect closet having taken shape, it's time to see how well it meshes with what's on the market. You can work with an architect or designer and create a one-of-a-kind closet that's

been tailored just for you. Semicustom systems offer a menu of prefabricated components that are assembled to fit an existing closet. Available through specialized storage retailers as well as from closet-organizer franchises, they are affordable and flexible. Finally there's the do-it-yourself approach, which often takes the form of basic kits of coated wire rods and shelves.

While organization experts generally caution against creating specialized storage suited for only one purpose, there are some locations in the home that are likely to function best if planned for a single need. Because most specialized storage, such as a CD rack, requires users to stash items in a certain way, it's ideal for spaces shared by the whole family, such as the television or media room. Specially designated storage works well in the foyer too, which must neatly accommodate the entire family's outerwear while still making a good first impression on guests.

Specialty

▌ work hard ▌ at play ▌

Specialized storage in areas such as the home office, foyer, and media or family room improves function, saves time, and maintains order.

talking trash

Some of the most frequently used, and therefore hardest working, areas of your home can benefit from dedicated, specialized storage. One such storage area is the recycling center. Depending on where it's located within your home, plan this area

work hard

to hold the items you regularly recycle in buckets, trash bins, or baskets. Then label each or develop a color-coding system. For example, even the smallest family members can follow a simple system, such as all plastics go in the blue container, paper in the white, trash in the green. You'll still need to maintain a collection area with larger containers. Ideally this is located outside the home or in or near the garage. Choose large bins on wheels if containers must be taken to the curb for pickup.

Trash and recycling bins are used several times each day during preparations for meals and snacks, so the location of each is an important consideration. The aim is to make recycling convenient. Then, it becomes less of a chore for the primary cook, and your family will find it easier to participate.

Here are some tips for making recycling an easy habit for all.

❙ Plan a cutout in the countertop that allows you to drop vegetable peels and other nonprotein food scraps into an undercounter bin. This bin can then be easily removed and carried out to the compost pile daily.

❙ Conserve time and motion, save floor space, and keep pets out of the trash by selecting concealed trash bins that tilt out or pull out on a platform installed on drawer slides. You'll find many configurations, including models that hide behind a single cabinet door and conceal from one to three bins, so you can recycle at the same spot where you dispose of trash.

❙ Choose four bins if local recycling requirements call for less mingling and more sorting of recycled items. But you'll need to stash these behind two cabinet doors, not one.

❙ Choose bins in sizes that suit how much recyclable trash you actually generate. A container that's too small will mean more trips to the outdoor recycling bins.

❙ Conserve space in the recycling bin by making a habit of flattening items like plastic bottles and cardboard packages.

❙ Keep the supply of extra trash bags at the bottom of the can underneath the bag you are currently using. You'll always have one handy when changing bags, and you will free up a little bit of drawer space for another item.

❙ Try to locate the trash anywhere but in the cabinet under the sink so that whoever does the dishes has an unobstructed place to stand and still gain access to it.

make recycling easy with

LEFT Rollers on this recycling bin allow you to tuck it under an island in the kitchen or easily stash it in the pantry, laundry, or mudroom.

BELOW LEFT Select the number of trash receptacles to include in your recycling center based on how your municipality requires that you sort the trash.

RIGHT Turn a kitchen island into a central recycling area by including rollout trash bins in the base cabinets.

OPPOSITE TOP Large, clearly labeled receptacles hold recyclables in the garage until collection day.

OPPOSITE BOTTOM Pullout front-to-back trash receptacles make use of the full depth of just one base cabinet for recycling.

bright idea

ergonomic

If your kitchen includes a pullout chopping board, consider installing a pullout trash bin in the cupboard below it. Sweep scraps directly into the trash as you work.

dedicated storage ||||||||||||||||||||||||||||||||||||||||||||||

Include plenty of hooks for items used on a daily basis. Make it easy for the kids to use the system by installing the hooks where they can reach.

A bench is handy as a resting spot for packages, purse, or briefcase, and invaluable on days when the weather requires wearing boots.

Designate a drawer for each family member to stash outerwear, keys, and the like.

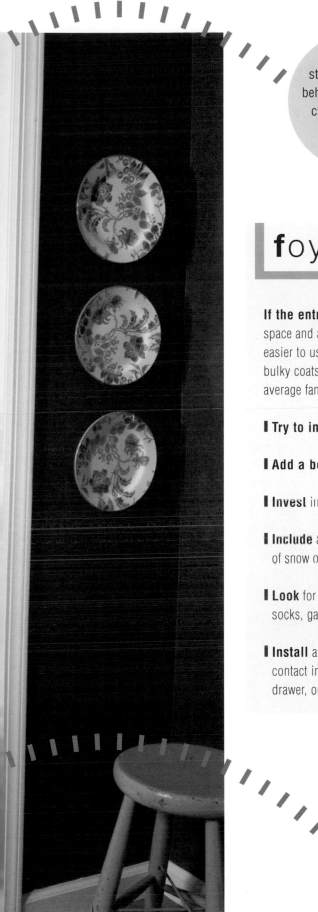

Plan some storage concealed behind doors to hide clutter and to put away out-of-season gear.

foyer and **m**udroom **i**deas

If the entry to your home is one of cluttered chaos, it is possible to reorganize the space and add storage to make it more functional. For example, the foyer or mudroom is easier to use and maintain if it includes storage dedicated to efficiently handling not only bulky coats but the myriad hats, gloves and mittens, boots, and shoes of all sizes that the average family collects. In the interest of neatness

❚ Try to include some enclosed hanging space in your foyer.

❚ Add a bench and individual cubbies or cabinets for each family member.

❚ Invest in a shoe rack to keep items such as sneakers and garden clogs neatly paired.

❚ Include a wall-mounted towel warmer, especially if you live in an area that receives lots of snow or rain. Use it to hang up wet coats, snowsuits, and mittens for fast, gentle drying.

❚ Look for a spot to stash a laundry basket in the mudroom to hold items such as damp socks, gardening clothes, sports uniforms, and pool towels.

❚ Install a bulletin board or a blackboard. Use it to post schedules and family members' contact information. Keep an extra set of keys to the tool shed and garage in a box, drawer, or basket in the foyer.

Choose a durable, waterproof finish material, such as stone or ceramic tile, for the floor in the foyer or mudroom.

sorting mail

A mail-sorting-and-recycling system set up in the foyer or mudroom (below) saves both time and steps, and it's an efficient way to eliminate clutter before it can gain a foothold in your house. With the current proliferation of promotional mailers, most households have pounds of unwanted paper delivered to their doors each day. Set up a mail-sorting-and-recycling center near the door where the mail is picked up and there's no need to clutter up a desk, table, or kitchen counter with junk mail, even temporarily.

❚ **Should you go through the mail** in the mudroom or the foyer? Which location you choose depends on where your mail is delivered. Many homeowners pick up their mail from a box located at the end of the driveway and enter the house via a side or back door, making the mudroom the best spot. Others return home through the front entry to pick up mail left in a box there and would find a foyer mail-sorting station most useful.

❚ **Start with a few stackable bins** in the mudroom or baskets stashed under a foyer console table. Even the drawers in an old desk or buffet can serve this function. Earmark one for recycling catalogs you don't want to keep, along with the colored-ink sections of the Sunday papers, too, if you are not a coupon clipper. Include another bin, basket, or drawer for catalogs

you will look at when time permits. Color-code or clearly label each so that you won't confuse them, or choose baskets with different colored or patterned liners. Next, toss junk mail and used envelopes in a wastebasket. You'll find many attractive models to suit all decors in a wide array of materials, including wood, rattan, wicker, and metal. Just be sure the container is large enough to handle the load from a few days. This collection can then be taken out the nearby door to a larger container for recycling or trash pickup.

❚ **In a more formal front entryway,** look for attractive containers, fabric-covered boxes, or fabric-lined baskets. Add a wall-hung hutch or cabinet with cubbies to leave mail for each family member. After you've trimmed down the pile, bring only the necessary pieces into the main part of the house.

TOP LEFT Add a mirror to the foyer furnishings so that you can do a last-minute grooming check before leaving the house.

MIDDLE LEFT Baskets are a great way to organize. Rather than using one large basket that too easily becomes a jumble, allocate one smaller basket per family member.

BOTTOM LEFT If the space in the foyer permits, include some long hanging storage behind closed doors, such as in a closet, locker, cabinet, or armoire.

BELOW This system uses tracks, wire hooks, and baskets to transform any wall into storage for coats and other gear.

create an illusion

Even if you do not have the room for a full foyer or mudroom, you can create the sense that there is one. Here are two ideas you can try:

▌**Find a chest of drawers** that fits the area just inside your main entry. Hang a mirror above, and if there is an electrical outlet nearby, put a small lamp on top.

▌**Use a simple bench.** Choose one with a lift-up lid and storage under the seat. Or stash baskets below and install pegs or hooks nearby. Complete the area with a mirror or message board.

LEFT Labeled bins and divided racks are valuable tools to keep track of many small items, such as the media stored in this professional photographer's office.

OPPOSITE Specialized storage, such as deep baskets, labeled boxes, see-through bins, and a rolling cart for art supplies, featured in this artist's office and studio help maintain order so that creativity can flourish.

increase productivity with an uncluttered office

ABOVE Specialize the storage in your home office to suit what you use there. For example, commodious baskets hold swatches and samples in a designer's home office.

RIGHT If your work does not require an entire room, a single piece of furniture can function as a compact yet efficient home office. This one offers plenty of specialized storage, including built-in pockets on the doors for files, a file drawer, pullout keyboard tray, and several adjustable shelves.

bright idea
arm's reach

Most people's reach extends no more than about 30 inches when seated at a desk. For efficiency and convenience, keep essential work tools and files for ongoing projects within that zone.

work at home

With the number of people who spend all or part of the work week at home steadily on the rise, the availability of products that can help turn any room in your home into an office has burgeoned. Shop in retail stores and specialty catalogs to find storage items that suit the style of your home and your work habits. Good storage will not only help you work more efficiently, it will keep the office from intruding on the serenity of your home and vice versa. Effective home-office organization and proper specialized-storage capabilities also prevent wasted time spent looking for (or worse yet, losing) important items or documents. Here are some additional tips to help you plan optimal office storage:

▌**Arrange** the furnishings so that you can reach as much of what you use on a daily basis as possible (phone, files, reference material) without leaving your chair. Keep in mind that an L-shaped desk arrangement is the most functional.

▌**Store** supplies in labeled boxes, baskets, or bins. Store backup supplies, such as extra paper and printer cartridges, tucked away in a closet.

▌**Avoid** wasted wall space. Extend shelves from the floor to the ceiling.

▌**Plan** on more drawers and shelves than you need right now to allow for expansion so that you don't outgrow your home office too quickly.

IIII portable storage to suit every need IIIIIIIIIIIIIIIIIIIIIIIIIII

OPPOSITE TOP LEFT Turn office walls into functional storage space with a wire shelving system designed for that purpose.

OPPOSITE TOP RIGHT Sturdy, divided rolling boxes are ideal for storing books that might otherwise be too large to fit on a standard-width shelf and too heavy to move easily.

LEFT Storing many small items grouped together in suitably sized containers makes them easier to retrieve.

OPPOSITE BOTTOM LEFT Shop hardware stores, home centers, and specialty retailers for drawer dividers. These handy inserts aid in keeping the contents organized so that small items are readily accessible. Tip: be sure to measure the drawers before you shop.

OPPOSITE BOTTOM RIGHT A rolling cart with several drawers offers flexible and portable storage for all kinds of office supplies. Tip: look for one that can store under the desk when not in use.

LEFT Clear, easily readable labels on storage boxes will save time when you need to find a particular item.

at play

Lack of adequate storage nearly always results in clutter. And clutter usually translates into chaos, which is not conducive to relaxation. That's why well-executed storage is as important in the play areas of the home as it is in the work areas. Why spend valuable free time needlessly hunting for the book you want to read or the CD you want to hear when good storage ensures that you can keep the items you use in your leisure time right at your fingertips? No matter how you choose to spend your free time—watching movies, listening to music, reading, cooking and entertaining, sewing, or crafting— well-organized spaces will help you get the most out of precious down time. Look for ways to store and catalog craft and hobby supplies, sports gear, games, music, movies, books, recipes, and even wines so that you can find what you want when you want it and spend your free time playing rather than hunting for an item.

media stats

When you're shopping for storage racks or other types of containment for your audio and video recordings, keep these standard measurements handy.

Audiocassette case	2¾ x 4¼ in.
Videocassette case	4⅛ x 7½ in.
CD case	5⅝ x 5 in.
LP-record sleeve	12⅜ x 12⅜ in.
DVD case	5⅜ x 7½ in.

bright idea

perfect

The ideal way to store media like CDs and DVDs is in shallow drawers just deep enough for one layer so that you can easily read labels.

OPPOSITE Custom-built cabinets are the most sophisticated way to store media components. Don't rush into expensive built-ins, though, until you're sure the system won't be changing radically or if you anticipate those changes and incorporate them into the design.

ABOVE AND TOP Now you see it, now you don't, when media and electronic components are hidden behind sliding doors. This is one way to conceal the TV in a room that must serve more than one purpose.

RIGHT Media storage can be as simple as a readily available over-the-door rack that allows you to stack a number of cases so that you can read the labels. Install the rack on the inside of a closet door so that the collection is out of sight but still nearby.

cabinets cleverly conceal components

LEFT AND ABOVE Audio components, a television, and a large plush sofa turn this room into a comfortable family viewing or listening space with the doors to the cabinets opened. With the doors closed, the focal point of the lofty space shifts to the wall with the fireplace and the colorful painting.

upgrading the experience

If you're thinking of creating a home theater, here are a few pointers:

▌ **Most home-theater designers** recommend television screens that are at least 27 in. wide.

▌ **Seating distance** is important for viewing quality. For optimal viewing, there should be a distance between you and the TV that is two to two and one-half times the width of the screen. If your TV is a wide-screen high-definition TV, place a distance that is one and one-half times the screen's diagonal width between you and it.

▌ **Five speakers** will create a full home-theater sound. Place one speaker on each side of the TV screen, level with your ears when you are seated and about 3 ft. from the sidewalls. Place two speakers behind the sofa about 6 to 8 ft. off the floor and at least as wide apart as the front speakers. Put the fifth speaker on top of the TV.

bright idea

swivel

If your television is not large and heavy, install it on a swivel platform. For the most comfortable viewing, turn the screen toward whatever seat you choose to use.

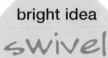

ABOVE LEFT AND RIGHT Retractable doors on the middle part of this unit slide back into the cabinet and allow an unobstructed view of the TV screen.

BELOW LEFT AND RIGHT Traditionally styled cabinetry not only conceals large electronic gear but also provides dedicated storage for tapes, CDs, DVDs, remote controls, and other entertainment gear.

RIGHT Solve book-storage issues by building cases that extend all the way to the ceiling. Then install a rolling-track library ladder to reach the highest shelves.

BELOW LEFT Proper lighting, such as adjustable track or recessed fixtures, installed above the front of the bookcases helps to illuminate the titles.

BELOW RIGHT If possible, it's best to locate bookcases so that they are not in direct sunlight.

organize the home library

the care of books

Here are some guidelines for keeping your library—whether it's an entire room lined with built-in bookcases or a single shelf unit next to a cozy chair—in good shape. Remember: books are sensitive to environmental factors.

❚ **Because humidity** and extreme temperatures are their enemies, try not to position bookcases against an outside wall, which is often prone to temperature fluctuations.

❚ **Shield books** from strong light (natural or artificial) to keep the bindings from fading.

❚ **To prevent warping,** stand books of like sizes together on a shelf packed neither too tightly nor too loosely.

❚ **Don't push books** all the way to the back of shelves where ventilation might be minimal; over time, mold could form.

❚ **Store fragile** or large and heavy volumes flat.

❚ **For an elegant touch,** display a particularly significant or attractive book on a stand.

bright idea

homebodies

Store books in the climate-controlled part of your home. The garage, basement, an unheated porch, or an attic are all disastrous for books —as is extended time in a cardboard box.

book **l**earning

Here are a few more tips to guarantee long life for your favorite books:

▌ **A collection of books** may start out small, but it usually grows, so plan shelves that are substantial enough to accommodate the weight of a full-grown library. In addition, because few book collections stay static, plan on some extra shelf space for expansion.

▌ **Store books** upright, if possible.

▌ **Overcrowding books** can damage them. Allow 1 in. of space between the top of the book and the next shelf above.

▌ **Create a stepped bookcase** with some shelves that are shallower than others (below). Use the shallow shelves for small books and paperbacks. Vary shelf depth from a low of 9 in. to 16 in.

ABOVE Books are best stored in an upright position in a climate-controlled space.

OPPOSITE TOP Plan some extra shelves so that you'll have room for the inevitable expansion of a book collection. Avoid jamming books into too-tight spaces. Better to sell or give away a few books than to risk damaging the bindings on all.

OPPOSITE BOTTOM Because bookcases are large features, they will likely dominate most spaces. Be sure the design fits the style of the home and the room where they are to be located.

bright idea

patience

If you paint bookshelves, check the manufacturer's label for curing time. Keep books off the shelves until paint has not only dried but also cured, which can take weeks.

|||||||conceal supplies

LEFT Look for attractive and imaginative containers that suit the decorative tone of your home to stash craft and hobby supplies. Cabinets or a freestanding piece of furniture with glass doors will allow you to easily see the contents but keep supplies or projects dust-free.

BELOW A long narrow table provides the workspace for an artist in a garage turned art studio.

OPPOSITE TOP Cabinets and deep drawers conceal backup supplies, while a rolling cart and several desktop containers hold materials and tools for the current project right on hand.

OPPOSITE BOTTOM LEFT Containers in every shape and size are readily available at home centers and storage retailers. Select clear models, and you can view the contents quickly. Use labels when possible.

OPPOSITE BOTTOM RIGHT Many crafters dream of a roomy closet dedicated to storing their supplies. Organizing stores of materials such as buttons, yarns, threads, and fabrics by color means you can quickly locate what's needed.

bright idea

creative space

When setting up a craft or hobby area, plan sufficient storage for supplies as well as for inspirational materials such as patterns, fabrics, photos, magazines, or personal treasures.

if craft and living areas share space ||||||||||||||||||||||||||||||

TOP LEFT A dedicated wine cellar might be your dream. It is not so farfetched if you have space in your basement to convert. Even though the basement is usually cool and damp, it's likely you'll need to invest in some climate-control equipment to maintain optimal temperature and humidity on a year-round basis.

LEFT Most cabinet manufacturers offer some form of bottle rack so that you can plan built-in wine storage that integrates well with your kitchen cabinetry.

ABOVE This cleverly designed wine-storage wall holds hundreds of bottles, yet takes up minimal floor space.

store wine away from heat and direct sunlight

ABOVE Wine coolers and refrigerators, like this space-saving undercounter model, hold several dozen bottles at optimal temperatures. Some larger models include separate red- and white-wine-storage sections.

BELOW Build a wine-holding area into the end of a cabinet run or an island.

Whether for sentimental, personal, or legal reasons there are some possessions that most people can't, or shouldn't, part with, and so must store for the long term. Wedding gowns, gently used clothing in good enough condition to hand down from one child to another, seasonal clothing, and sports gear likely top many lists. Other probable long-term storage items found in many homes include tax records, photographs, family keepsakes or heirlooms, legal documents, children's artwork, and collections. This chapter offers ideas about how to correctly store a variety of these items over time.

Long-Term

I keepsakes I
I documents and valuables I
I basement and attic I
I seasonal I

Check storage and specialty retailers' shelves and catalogs for products that are safe to use for long-term storage of important documents and precious keepsakes.

fabric facts

Family heirlooms often include a variety of fabric items. Here are some tips for storing them for the long term:

▌ **Make sure fabrics** are clean and completely dry before packing them away.

▌ **Wash garments** with a scent-free detergent before storing. Put them through an extra rinse (or even two) to be sure all traces of detergent residue are gone.

▌ **Never store fabrics** in plastic bags. Plastic can trap moisture and lead to mildew.

▌ **The acid in wood hangers** or the drawer of a break-front or bureau will eventually harm fabrics. For this reason, do not hang garments on wooden hangers for long-term storage, either. Instead, wrap family heirlooms, such as christening or wedding gowns and veils, in acid-free tissue paper, or pack them in acid-free cardboard boxes specially made for long-term fabric storage before placing them in a drawer.

▌ **Long-term hanging** can weaken fabric fibers. It's better to store fabric items, loosely folded and wrapped in acid-free tissue, in an acid-free cardboard box.

▌ **Over time,** standard cardboard boxes also leach acid from the organic matter used to make them. The only safe long-term storage for heirloom fabrics (as well as for photographs and books) is acid-free boxes, which are readily available through storage retailers.

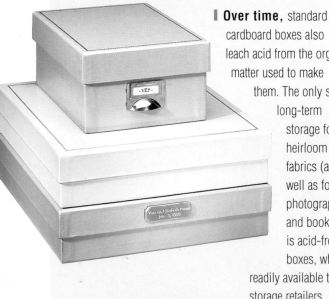

keepsakes

TOP Purchase archival albums and storage boxes to safeguard one-of-a-kind keepsake photos.

ABOVE It's a good idea to review photos and other collections at least once a year to check for signs of deterioration.

OPPOSITE Keep photos that are on display out of direct sunlight.

bright idea

photo smart

If you are the steward of precious heirloom photos, display a copy and not the original. Store original photographs in a safe or safe-deposit box, encased in protective sleeves and boxes.

A keepsake is any item with either historical or sentimental meaning to you or a family member. A hand-knit blanket your grandmother made for your firstborn; a child's favorite, but now outgrown, toys; a lace veil worn by generations of family brides; your son's mementoes from summer camp; family furniture or silver; photographs; and letters all could be defined as keepsakes. And all will require thoughtful handling to store properly and preserve. Because the materials that keepsakes are made of vary so widely, they are likely to require different types of storage.

bright idea
media

Contact your local photo lab or camera store about transferring videotapes or irreplaceable photographs currently stored on film to DVD format to preserve them for the long-term.

❚❚❚❚ display keepsakes and heirlooms carefully ❚❚❚❚❚❚❚❚❚❚❚

ABOVE Sometimes long-term storage means keeping an item, such as this collection of antique medallions, out in view on display.

LEFT Display vintage garments for only short periods if you wish to preserve them. Avoid long-term hanging and contact with wood or metal hooks and hangers because this stresses and damages fibers.

fabrics

Fabric items, such as table linens, that are properly cared for and stored can last for generations. Here are some basic care tips:

▌**Natural-fiber table linens,** including cloths and napkins made of cotton, silk, or linen, are susceptible to decay and mold, so they should be stored in a dry place away from light and dust. Left untreated, stains will set while in storage, so put away only freshly laundered and ironed linens.

▌**Fold linens neatly** before putting them in drawers. To protect fragile fabrics against yellowing, interleave them with sheets of acid-free tissue paper, available in retail stores, online, or by mail order.

▌**To minimize wrinkles,** drape table runners and cloths over a padded (preferable) or sturdy wooden hanger before hanging them. For more protection, store them in a garment bag. Cushion the hanger or the rods with a few folded sheets of archival (acid-free) tissue paper to deter creases and to prevent the hanger from staining the fabric. Don't let the fabric puddle at the bottom, or you'll be doing some last-minute ironing before your dinner party. If you can't hang them, fold them neatly in a shallow acid-free box or wrap them in tissue paper. Another option: launder but don't iron items until just before using them. Sometimes all you have to do to eliminate minor wrinkles is spritz the cloth with a little cold water and place it in the clothes dryer, set on wrinkle-free, for a few minutes.

ABOVE If you own a collection of vintage quilts or fabrics and want to display them, hang them out of direct light and periodically rotate the items you show.

storage and the photograph

Treat your family photographs like valuable objects. While most snapshots need only be stored in an album or box to prevent them from being lost, bent, or creased, photographs that are valued for historic, artistic, or personal reasons are once-in-a-lifetime, one-of-a-kind objects. When you look for a storage spot for photos within your home, think cool, dark, and dry.

Avoid popular off-the-shelf methods of storing photographs such as magnetic or black-paper albums and scrapbooks. Unless labeled "archival," "lignin-free," "neutral Ph," or "acid-free," they contain chemicals that will eventually harm the photographs. Shop for photo-storage items in a camera or photo shop or from catalogs and retailers that specialize in archival products. (See the Resource Guide.)

Store prints, as well as negatives, in plastic sleeves that have the word "archival" printed somewhere on them.

Think about using black-and-white film when you take photos. Or consider converting some of your important photographs into black-and-white prints. Black-and-white photography lasts longer than color. Due to unavoidable chemical reactions and dye changes, no color pictures are permanent.

❚ **Be careful** with negatives and original transparencies, because these are the only way to reprint copies. Scratches, light, and dirt can damage negatives that are not stored in sleeves or envelopes. Store black-and-white negatives separately from color negatives and slides away from all negatives. Store negatives in chemically inert archival plastic sleeves or in acid-free envelopes.

❚ **Wash your hands** before handling negatives, and touch them at the edges only. Never touch the face of the negative because oils from your skin will damage it.

❚ **Never keep a photograph** that has begun to deteriorate in a box with photographs that are in good condition.

❚ **Keep photos** out of light. Any visible light, not just sunlight, fades photographs. If you display photographs, do not put them in direct sunlight and do not shine artificial light directly on them.

❚ **Store photographs** and negatives where the temperature is constant. Cooler temperatures are better, so do not put photos in the attic for long-term storage. Be careful not to store photo albums near heat ducts.

❚ **Keep humidity** at no more than 50 percent. Avoid damp basements, laundry rooms, and bathrooms, and watch out for overhead water pipes, sprinkler systems, and toilets on the floor above the storage area.

❚ **Rotate the photos** you keep out on display on a regular basis.

❚ **Review your photos** at least once a year. While you are enjoying the collection, check for fading, deterioration, and mildew, as well as insect damage.

IIII fragile items benefit from extra care IIIIIIIIIIIIIIIIIIIIIII

bright idea

maintain

Items stored on long-term display demand upkeep. Wash crystal and glassware regularly so that they stay their sparkling best.

ABOVE Crystal is more prone to scratches than regular glassware. Never store anything inside a crystal pitcher or vase. And store glasses standing upright, not on the rim.

ABOVE RIGHT Purchase zippered cases specially designed to protect china and other fragile items while in storage. These relatively inexpensive devices protect plate rims and keep contents dust-free.

RIGHT Wrap silver pieces in anti-tarnish felt bags, or buy a do-it-yourself kit for lining drawers with anti-tarnish felt.

OPPOSITE Before displaying fragile pottery, china, or glassware, be certain shelves are sturdy enough to support the weight of the collection.

china and glass

▌**Throw out chipped or cracked china or glass**. Repeat the procedure for stained tablecloths and napkin or placemat sets that are incomplete, out of fashion, faded, or worn. Not only will this free up more storage space, but with the damaged goods out of the picture you will be able to assess your replacement and storage needs with accuracy.

▌**Rather than wait for the night** before the family feast, make it a rainy-day activity to polish the silverware and wash and press the napery. Remember: silver must be completely dry before it can be put away.

▌**Keep your china together by pattern** (if you have more than one). Separate serving pieces from place settings. Then within each pattern, sort by size: all dinner plates, salad plates, dessert plates, soup bowls or coupes, cups, mugs, and saucers. Do the same with your silverware, stemware, and glasses.

▌**Draw up a list** of how many of each piece you have. Then use it as the basis for making or buying the correct number of appropriately sized storage accessories.

bright idea

be sure

Even with a burglar-resistant safe, it's wise to install a monitored alarm system. With enough time, a burglar can break into almost any safe. An alarm reduces the time he can work undetected.

documents and valuables

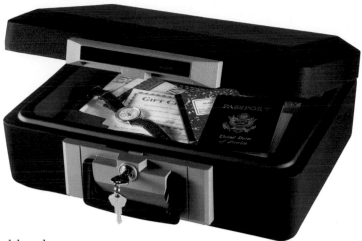

Take an inventory of exactly how many valuable photos, irreplaceable documents, and treasured pieces of jewelry you need to store. Next, decide on which storage device will work best, keeping in mind that valuables optimally need protection not only from theft but also from fire and water. Options include metal storage containers, such as safes, chests, or files. Evaluate the possibilities by looking at features such as the thickness of the steel; whether the lock is a standard combination, easy-to-use keypad, or state-of-the-art biometric; and the ability to customize the interior organization. At the least costly end of the spectrum, your local locksmith or hardware store likely offers small storage containers designed to safeguard valuables from theft. These appear to be ordinary food and household product containers, such as cleaning supplies and toiletries, but are actually hollow containers that you can fill with valuables and store at the rear of the pantry or supply closet shelf.

safeguard

Here's a list of what you might store in a well-rated fire- and waterproof safe.

- Birth certificates
- Immunization records
- Cherished photos
- Tax documents
- Wills
- Passports
- Titles and registrations
- Investment records
- Insurance paperwork
- Bank records
- Mortgage papers
- Deeds
- Home inventory list
- Marriage license or certificate
- Divorce documents
- Custody paperwork
- Contracts
- Receipts for large-ticket items
- Spare keys
- Owner's manuals
- Religious documents
- Jewelry
- Stocks and bonds
- Collectibles
- Mementos

OPPOSITE TOP LEFT Clever storage devices, such as floor safes, are readily available at hardware stores and locksmith shops. However, be aware that some do not provide protection from fire or water damage.

OPPOSITE TOP RIGHT Browse archival storage product catalogs for devices, such as polyethylene bags, that offer some protection for collectibles from dust, moisture, and pollution.

OPPOSITE BOTTOM For the best fire and theft protection, buy a safe based on its weight and the thickness of the walls. Be sure it is fire-rated to withstand temperatures high enough to protect what you plan to store there.

ABOVE Check for an independent third-party evaluation on protection devices, such as storage safes, chests, or files, that claim to be fire-resistant. Third-party evaluations verify that the manufacturer's claims are accurate.

LEFT Keep certain household files, such as appliance use-and-care guides or warranties and service contracts, available for quick reference in a file drawer in the kitchen.

BELOW Use sturdy reinforced divided boxes, such as those shown, to safely store china and glassware for the long term. A rolling cart will help you move heavy items when you need to relocate or use the contents.

storage boxes for every need

filing facts

Choose filing cabinets based on the value and quantity of what you will be storing.

▎**Set files up with a system** that makes sense to you. Divide drawers by broad categories, and file by function. One simple organizing tool: color-coded file folders. For a quick and easy point of reference, choose a different color for each category. And label all folders clearly with block-printed letters in a nons-mearing, waterproof ink. File the newest items at the front of the folder, keeping the oldest ones at the back.

▎**File folders are most efficient** to use if you hang them in a rack that clearly shows off the label. Files that are stacked quickly become a jumble.

▎**Weed dead files out** of the active filing system and then out of your office as promptly as possible. Transfer them into cardboard banker's boxes; label and date them; and send them to the great filing cabinet in the sky (the attic, of course). Once a year, review these archives and throw out the boxes that hold papers that no longer have a use.

RIGHT If you work at home in a basement or grade-level space, store files in metal cabinets with a toekick high enough to raise the drawers at least a few inches off the floor. Select file cabinets with a high fire rating if your business would be devastated by losing the files.

BELOW RIGHT Use attractive wicker file baskets to organize loose paperwork and turn any space into a hardworking home office.

No matter where you plan to put things, you'll need to get the storage areas in the basement and attic in shape before you do anything. Tackle the areas separately, and be prepared to spend at least one weekend working on each one. Don't move from one to the next until you are finished.

Do a thorough clean out. If you can't face the thought of doing it all at once, set a timer for an hour at a time and clear one shelf, corner, or drawer at each session. Don't move on until you are finished.

Plan proper disposal. Be sure to check with your local sanitation department about special regulations involving the disposal of chemicals, computers, appliances, batter-

basement and attic

ies, or thermometers, among other things, that contain environmentally harmful or recyclable materials. Decide ahead of time what you will do with the usable items you no longer want. As you are cleaning out the space, organize things into sell, trash, donate, or give-to stacks.

Bring the space up to par. Use this opportunity to do spot repairs, such as insulating exposed pipes in the basement; fixing a cracked window in the attic; improving the lighting; or adding electrical outlets. Sweeping and scrubbing will deter insects. Discourage rodents by stuffing steel wool into potential entries. In the end, these improvements will significantly upgrade the storage environment and, indeed, your home. And your belongings will be protected from damage or ruin.

Measure the room, paying particular attention to window locations and changes in ceiling and wall heights. Openings and entries to these areas may be smaller than those elsewhere in the house.

keep track

To keep track of long-term storage items, make diagrams of the attic and basement that illustrate their contents and the general location of items within the room: holiday decorations in the southeast quadrant; camping equipment midway on the north wall; and so on, for example. When you use, move, or discard items, update the diagrams as necessary. Post the map at the entrance to each space, and keep an extra set of copies in the kitchen or home office for a quick on-the-spot reference.

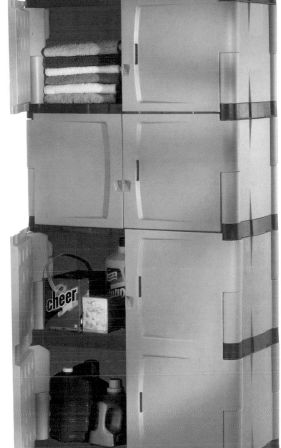

OPPOSITE Maximize attic space that might otherwise be wasted. These built-in drawers make full use of the hard-to-use space under the eaves.

ABOVE Hooks, cubbies, and a bench create a functional entry near a grade-level door.

ABOVE RIGHT Expand storage easily with this ready-made utilitarian cabinet.

RIGHT Use a dehumidifier in basement areas, where dampness could adversely affect stored items.

ABOVE Shop for systems designed to stretch storage space in your garage to accommodate objects as large as this kayak.

BELOW The owners of this ski house made it easy to stow gear correctly and keep it in good condition by providing a dedicated rack for skis and poles as well as a bench where skiers can stash boots.

Storing seasonal items so that they are safe yet accessible presents challenges in most homes. Because your possessions, such as holiday decorations, sporting gear, and out-of-season clothing, may be in use for only a short period, it's wise to store them in less-accessible areas when they are not in use. Though not all seasonal items are large and bulky, many are, and so

seasonal

they not only take up lots of space, but also might be difficult to maneuver into the farthest corners. One solution: investigate the array of products designed to turn the garage or basement walls into efficient storage. Add shelves or clothes poles in the higher reaches of closets, attics, and garages. Another option: purchase sturdy, out-size plastic bins, or perhaps build a shed to handle bulky seasonal items.

Unless all the closets in your home are huge walk-ins or you live in a single-season climate, it's likely the semiannual wardrobe changes present another challenge. Purge closets of ill-fitting, faded, and torn clothing, or items stained beyond repair at the end of each season. If you or your child did not wear an item this season, in all likelihood you will not wear it next year. If the item is serviceable, give it away. If not, throw it out. Prevent permanent stains and insect damage. Clean all items before storing them in one of the many bins and boxes you'll find at retailers and in catalogs. Finally, label each box so that you can easily find what you want when the next seasonal change rolls around.

TOP Even a small shed could provide instant storage relief. Sporting gear and toys stashed here are accessible in summer and safe from the effects of the harsh weather in winter.

BELOW Home centers and hardware stores offer an array of sturdy plastic bins that are ideal for sport, garden, and barbecue gear.

|||| keep garden gear accessible all year

ABOVE LEFT A grid-and-hook system, such as the one shown here, offers the flexibility to easily move items to a new location as the need arises.

ABOVE RIGHT During the season, this cart accompanies the gardener on rounds. In the winter months, tuck it into a corner of the garage or shed. Tip: wash tools and gloves before storing them long-term so that the acid in soil does not destroy them.

LEFT Save the garden hose to use for another season. As winter approaches, disconnect it and drain out all the water. Roll the hose neatly, and hang it on a large hook inside the garage to protect it from the freeze and thaw cycles of winter.

ABOVE AND RIGHT Set aside all decorations and holiday wrappings in a single location in the attic or basement. Use durable plastic or compartmentalized cardboard boxes to protect delicate ornaments. Then pad or fill any voids for further protection.

the family emergency kit

One item every family should have on hand in accessible yet long-term storage is an emergency preparedness kit. Gather the items from the list below in a large plastic bin clearly marked "emergency kit," and store it in the pantry or a closet that's not out of the way and located above the basement level. Check several times a year to be sure food and water are not outdated and that batteries are still good. Include the following:

❚ **Sufficient bottled water** (in plastic containers) to last at least three days for each person, as well as water for pets. Plan on one gallon per person per day.

❚ **Nutritious foods** that can be eaten without heating or cooking, such as canned and dried fruits, nuts, or seeds; nut butters; crackers; cereal; milk; canned fish; and beans. Don't forget pet food.

❚ **One complete change of clothing** for each family member, including socks and footwear.

❚ **Other basics, such as a first-aid kit** and a backup supply of medications and extra prescriptions, if possible; tools, such as a hammer, screwdriver, and wrench; a flashlight and a battery-powered radio, along with several sets of batteries for each; a scissor; candles; matches; toiletry articles; a can and bottle opener; and packaged moist hand wipes.

❚ **Enough cash** to fill your gas tank several times, at a minimum; a map of your area; and a list of important contacts or a copy of your address book.

❚ **Though not a necessity,** a deck of cards and some board games could help to keep your family occupied and reduce anxiety in an emergency that lasts for more than a few hours.

BELOW The summer potting shed can become the winter garden-tool storehouse. Add a pegboard and hooks to increase wall storage.

shed safety

The following safety checklist is worth reviewing. It was compiled by the Home Safety Council (homesafetycouncil.org), a non-profit, industry-supported group organized to help prevent injuries in the home.

▌**Organize all items you plan to store** in your shed in designated, easy-to-reach places, so large piles don't accumulate.

▌**Store shovels, rakes, lawn chairs,** bikes, and other sharp and large objects on the wall to prevent trips and falls.

▌**Keep children's playthings** in one area and within their reach to prevent young ones from exploring potentially dangerous areas.

▌**Make sure poisonous products** such as pesticides, automotive fluids, lighter fluid, paint thinner, antifreeze, and turpentine have child-resistant caps, are clearly labeled, and are stored either on a high shelf or, better yet, where kids can not access them—in a locked cabinet.

▌**Store gasoline in small quantities** only and in proper, tightly sealed containers labeled "gasoline."

▌**Store pool chemicals** according to the manufacturers' directions to prevent combustion and potential poisoning exposures.

▌**Properly secure shelving units** to the wall, making sure they are not overloaded, and keep heavier items closest to the ground.

▌**Keep a sturdy collapsible step stool** within easy access to help you reach items that are stored high on a shelf.

RIGHT What looks to be simply an attractive garden folly can be more than ornamentation. Plan a small shed, such as the one shown here, to hold garden tools and supplies.

❙❙❙❙ stretch storage with a shed ❙❙❙❙❙❙❙❙❙❙❙❙❙❙❙❙❙❙❙❙❙❙❙❙❙❙❙❙❙❙❙❙❙❙❙❙❙❙❙

sheds from **k**its

If you don't need a custom shed but just a utilitarian box for storing tools and equipment, a shed kit is a cost-efficient alternative. Typical kits for equipment sheds are simple structures with gable roofs that measure anywhere from about 4 x 5 ft. to 10 x 17 ft. Floor-to-ceiling clearance is usually 6 or 7 ft.

❙ **Wood kits generally** come with all the lumber precut, as well as enough fasteners to complete the project. Many styles are available. You can choose the cheapest, finished with T1-11 siding, or pick a kit with a siding similar to that of your house. Kits with metal siding and roof panels—usually steel with a baked-on enamel finish—are also available in a variety of styles. There are even sheds that look like a miniature version of a typical red-and-white gambrel barn.

❙ **Metal kits** are designed to be simple to assemble. Most parts snap together and are further strengthened with sheet-metal screws. The kits include prehung doors and other fixtures, but you still have to build the foundation. Because small metal buildings are light, they must be anchored to the foundation. In many regions, these sheds are considered permanent structures, and you will need to check installation details with your building department.

ABOVE LEFT AND RIGHT A hinged bench with drawers was incorporated into this run of kitchen cabinetry. Deep and wide, it can handle all kinds of stored items, from kitchen gear to household files or kids' toys.

LEFT AND BELOW Installed on the countertop, a deep, two-tiered drawer can be fitted for flatware and other utensils or a built-in spice rack.

llllllllllllllllll **look for new ways to organize your life** llllllllll

RIGHT Even shallow space should be considered when you're looking for extra storage. Here, it provides suitable housing for glassware.

BELOW Smart space planning gets the credit for this beverage center, which is located in a hallway just outside the dining room and kitchen of the home. It's been fitted with built-in cabinetry that holds servingware, a bar-size sink, and a wine cabinet, which can be used to chill soft drinks, too.

bright idea

out-of-the-way station

Compartmentalize space. A good example is a beverage center, which can be located anywhere. Install an under-counter refrigerator or refrigerated drawers, an ice maker, and wine storage.

Glossary

Knockdown: Having precut and prefit components; usually refers to unfinished furniture.

Lazy Susan: A shelf that rotates 360 degrees.

Level: The term used to define a surface or line that is perfectly horizontal. Also, the name given to a variety of instruments used to determine whether a surface or line is perfectly horizontal.

Miter: An angle cut into the face or thickness of a piece of lumber or other material to form a miter joint.

Miter Box: A wood, plastic, or metal jig with a saw, designed to manually cut wood at various angles.

Modular: Units of a standard size, such as pieces of a cabinet or wall system, that can be fitted together.

Molding: Decorative strips of wood or plastic used in various kinds of trimwork.

Molding: An architectural band used to trim a line where materials join, or to create a linear decoration. It is typically made of wood, plaster, or a polymer.

Mortise-and-Tenon Joinery: A joint in which a hole (mortise) is cut into one piece of wood to receive a projecting piece (tenon) cut into another.

Murphy Bed: A bed that folds into the wall or a closet when not in use.

Occasional Piece: A small piece of furniture for incidental use, such as an end table.

Orientation: The placement of any object or space, such as a window, a door, or a room, and its relationship to the points on a compass.

Panel: A flat, rectangular piece of material that forms part of a wall, door, or cabinet. Typically made of wood, it is usually framed by a border and either raised or recessed.

Pilaster: A vertical relief molding attached to a wall or cabinet, usually made to resemble the surface of a pillar.

Pillar: A column stretching from the floor or other support base to the ceiling or header above a passageway.

Platform Bed: A bed that features a mattress that rests on a platform that is over a bank of drawers.

Plumb: An expression describing a perfectly vertical surface or line. A plumb surface will meet a level surface at 90 degrees to form a right angle.

Pocket Door: A door that slides into the wall when it is open.

Prehung Door: A door that is already set in a jamb, with hinges preinstalled, really to be installed in a rough opening.

Proportion: The relationship of one object to another.

Pullout: A full-extension cabinet, such as a built-in pantry or hamper, basket, or shelf that is fitted with ball-bearing slides.

Rail System: A series of metal rails that are attached to a kitchen backsplash for the purpose of hanging small cooking utensils, such as ladles or tongs. Some sets come with S-hooks, hanging bins, knife racks, or small shelves.

Rod System: See "Rail System."

Scale: The size of a room or object.

Sideboard: A dining-room cabinet that is similar in size to a console table and has drawers for silverware and other flat articles.

Some sideboards come with lockable cupboards for storing valuables or sterling silver.

Sight Line: The natural line of sight the eye travels when looking into or around a room.

Slide-Out: See "Pullout."

Slope: The rise of a roof over its run, expressed as the number of inches of rise per unit of run (usually 12 inches).

Soffit: A boxed-in area just below the ceiling and above a cabinet.

Softwood: Generally, the wood of coniferous, needle-bearing trees such as pine, fir, or spruce.

Space Configuration: A design term that is used to describe the reallocation of interior space without adding on.

Spice Rack: A small cabinet or rack that can be freestanding on a countertop or mounted to a wall or interior cabinet door and used for storing bottled seasonings and spices.

Stud: A vertical support element made of wood or metal that is used in the construction of walls.

Surround: The tile or acrylic enclosure around a tub or shower.

Tambour Door: A cabinet door that is on a track and rolls up or down.

Task Lighting: Lighting that concentrates in specific areas for tasks, such as preparing food, applying makeup, reading, or doing crafts.

Tilt-Down Tray: The hinged, flat panel in front of the sink that tilts down to reveal a small storage pocket.

Toekick Drawer: A shallow drawer built into the recessed area below a cabinet. It can be used to store flat objects, such as a collapsible stool, cookie sheets, pamphlets, or stationery.

Tongue-and-Groove Joinery: A joinery technique in which a protruding end (tongue) fits into a recess (groove), locking the two pieces together.

Track Lighting: Lighting that utilizes a fixed band to carry electrical current and hold movable light fixtures.

Uplight: Also used to describe the lights themselves, this is actually the term for light that is directed upward toward the ceiling.

Valet Stand: A wooden or metal floor rack that is about the size of a wooden chair. It is used to hang a suit or jacket.

Vanity: A bathroom floor cabinet that usually contains sink and storage space.

Veneer: High-quality wood that is cut into very thin sheets for use as a surface material.

Vintage: Anything that is at least 20-25 years old, but not antique (at least 100 years old).

Wainscoting: Any trim structure installed in the area between a baseboard and a chair rail.

Photo Credits

All illustrations by Robert LaPointe

page 1: Tria Giovan page 3: carolynbates.com, architect: Frederick W. Horton page 4: Pizzi/Thompson, design: Maude & Scott MacGillivray page 6: *top left* Eric Roth, design: Easy Closets; *right* Mark Samu; *bottom left* Lucinda Symons/Retna.com pages 8–9: Stickley Photo•Graphic, design: KL Design page 10: Pizzi/Thompson, design: Seattle Design Build page 11: *top* Mark Samu; *bottom* Jessie Walker, design: Carol R. Knott, ASID page 12: Pizzi/Thompson, design: Jean Steinbrecher, AIA page 13: *top* K. Rice/Robertstock.com; *bottom* Stickley Photo•Graphic, design: Olson & Jones Construction page 14: *top* Index Open; *bottom* Phillip H. Ennis Photography page 15: *top left* Eric Roth; *top right* Tria Giovan; *bottom* Mark Samu page 16: *top left* Mark Samu, architect: Ellen Roche; *top right* Tony Giammarino/Giammarino & Dworkin; *bottom right* Jessie Walker, design: Neff Design Center; *bottom left* Mark Samu page 17: Phillip H. Ennis Photography page 18: *top left* Mark Samu; *top right* Tria Giovan; *bottom* Mark Samu page 19: *top* alanshortall.com; *bottom* carolynbates.com, architect: Allan Todd Koster page 20: Eric Roth, design: Easy Closets page 21: *top* Eric Roth; *bottom right* Mark Samu, design: Margaret McNicholas; *bottom left* Lisa Masson, design: Cabinets by American Woodmark page 22: Peter Tata, design: Carol Dishman of Diva page 23: Stickley Photo•Graphic, design: KL Design pages 24–25: *left* courtesy of Merillat; *center* Mark Samu; *right* courtesy of Toto pages 25–26: *left* Mark Samu; *center* courtesy of Robern; *right* Brian Vanden Brink, builder: Morningstar Marble & Granite page 28: *top* courtesy of Kraftmaid Cabinetry; *bottom right* Bob Greenspan, stylist: Susan Andrews; *bottom left* courtesy of Kraftmaid Cabinetry page 29: courtesy of Robern page 30: Tria Giovan page 31: *left* Tony Giammarino/Giammarino & Dworkin, design: Christina Hoppe; *top right* carolynbates.com, architect: Wendy Kohn; *bottom right* courtesy of Merillat page 32: *top right* Pizzi/Thompson, design: Maude & Scott MacGillivray; *top left* Brian Vanden Brink, architect: Polhemus Savery DaSilva Architects; *bottom* courtesy of IKEA page 33: courtesy of Elfa/The Container Store page 34: *top* courtesy of IKEA; *bottom* Brian Vanden Brink, architect: Whitten Winkleman Architects page 35: Mark Lohman, design: Janet Lohman pages 36–37: *all* Eric Roth, design: Easy

Closets pages 38–39: Tria Giovan page 40: *top* carolynbates.com, architect: Frank Lloyd Wright; *bottom* Tony Giammarino/Giammarino & Dworkin, design: Galeski page 41: Eric Roth, stylist: Ann Fitzgerald of Team Agency pages 42–43: *top left* Jessie Walker, design: Linda Brown; *top right* Jessie Walker, design: Dave McFadden; *bottom right* www.carolynbates.com, architect: Allan Todd Koster; *bottom left* Tony Giammarino/Giammarino & Dworkin page 44: *top left* Mark Samu, design: Kitchen Designs by Ken Kelley; *top right* Jessie Walker, design: Carol R. Knott, ASID; *bottom* carolynbates.com, architect: Brad Rabinowitz page 45: Eric Roth, architect: Catalano Architects page 48: *top* carolynbates.com; *bottom* Tria Giovan page 49: *top* Jessie Walker, design: Gayla Bailey; *bottom* ACE Photo Agency/Robertstock.com pages 50–51: *top* Jessie Walker, design: Barbara Horwich; *bottom right* Lisa Masson, design: Thomas Pheasant; *bottom center* Jessie Walker; *bottom left* Tony Giammarino page 52: *top* Stickley Photo•Graphic, design: Jan Kavale Interior Designs; *bottom* Jessie Walker page 53: Robertstock.com page 54: *left* Jessie Walker, design: David T. Smith; *right* Tony Giammarino, design: Lynn Avenoso page 55: *top* melabee m miller, design: Hope Sferra Interiors, Inc; *bottom* Jessie Walker, design: Barbara Metzler pages 56–57: *top left & top center* Lisa Masson; *bottom center* Lisa Masson, collector: Cozy Baker; *right & bottom left* Bradley Olman pages 58–59: Jessie Walker, architect: Tom Swartout page 60: *top* Russ Widstrand, design: City Cabinetmakers; *bottom* Bradley Olman page 61: Bradley Olman page 62: Stickley Photo•Graphic page 63: *left* Pizzi/Thompson, design: Janis Mumford; *right* Tria Giovan pages 64–65: *top right* Mark Samu, design: KJS Interiors; *bottom right* melabee m miller, design: Michelle Koenig, I.D.S., ASID/Bruchele Interiors; *bottom left* Russ Widstrand, design: City Cabinetmakers; *top center* Pizzi/Thompson, design: French Tradition page 66: *top* melabee m miller, design: Sharon Draznin; *bottom* Roger Turk, architect: Roger Katz Architects page 67: *top* K. Rice/Robertstock.com; *bottom* Jessie Walker, design: Dave McFadden page 68: Jessie Walker, architect: Richard Becker page 69: *right* Jessie Walker; *bottom left* carolynbates.com; *top left* carolynbates.com, design: Milford Cushman/The Cushman Design Group, Inc. page 70: *top* Mark Samu, architect: Brian Shore, AIA; *bottom* Jessie Walker page 71: *right* Pizzi/Thompson, design:

Jean Steinbrecher; *bottom left* Phillip H. Ennis Photography, design: Salem Hill Studio; *top left* Pizzi/Thompson page 72: *top right* Jessie Walker, design: Barbara Horwich; *bottom* carolynbates.com, design: The Snyder Companies/Snyder Group, Inc.; *top left* Jessie Walker page 73: Mark Samu, custom cabinets design: Carpen House, Inc. page 74: *top* Phillip H. Ennis Photography, design: Linda Shockly Interiors; *bottom* Pizzi/Thompson, design: Chris Soderberg & Ann Laman page 75: *top right* Pizzi/Thompson, design: Rochelle Carmona; *bottom right* Lisa Masson, builder: C. Hughes; *left* carolynbates.com, architect: Malcolm Appleton/Architectural Association page 76: *top* Phillip H. Ennis Photography, design: Interior Consultants; *bottom* Roger Turk, builder: Gary Howe Construction page 77: Phillip H. Ennis Photography, design: Bradley Thiergartner Designs page 80: *top* Pizzi/Thompson, design: Linda & Gordon Davis/Saltbox Sampler; *bottom* Pizzi/ Thompson, design: Shirley Christiansen Interiors page 81: *top* Eric Roth; *bottom* Jessie Walker, design: Barbara Metzler page 82: *top* carolynbates.com, design: Mitra Design, builder: Conner & Buck Builders; *bottom* Phillip H. Ennis Photography, architect: Chary & Siquenza Architects page 83: *top* Roger Turk, architect: Todd Soli Architects; *bottom* Stickley Photo•Graphic pages 84–85: *top right* Eric Roth; *bottom right* Tria Giovan; *bottom center* Pizzi/Thompson, design: Jean Steinbrecher; *left* Pizzi/Thompson, design: Marilyn & Peter Grossman; *top center* Mark Samu page 87: *top* Jessie Walker, design: Liz Kavanaugh; *bottom* Jessie Walker, design: Cornerstone Builders page 88: *top right* K. Rice/Robertstock.com; *bottom right* melabee m miller, design: Virginia Smith; *top left* Pizzi/Thompson, design: Seattle Design Build page 89: *top* carolynbates.com, architect: Roland Batten/Lynda McIntyre; *bottom* A. Teufen/Robertstock.com pages 90–91: Christopher Drake/Retna.com pages 92–93: *clockwise from top right* courtesy of Ballard Designs; courtesy of Ballard Designs; courtesy of Ethan Allen; Lisa Masson, design: Linda Stotts pages 94–95: *top left* Lisa Masson, design: Marilyn Poling; *top center* Russell Sadur/Retna.com; *right* Christl Roehl/Retna.com; *bottom center* Tony Giammarino/Giammarino & Dworkin page 96: Jessie Walker, design: Blair Baby page 97: *top* Jessie Walker, design: Dave McFadden; *bottom right* courtesy of Ethan Allen; *bottom left* Robertstock.com page 98: courtesy of Ethan

Allen **page 99:** *top* Lucinda Symons/Retna.com; *bottom* Winfried Heinz/Retna.com **pages 100–101:** *top* Lucinda Symons/Retna.com; *bottom right* Stewart Grant/Retna.com; *bottom center* Pizzi/Thompson, design: Tom Callaway; *bottom left* courtesy of Ballard Designs **page 102:** Lucinda Symons/Retna.com **pages 103–104:** *all* courtesy of Ballard Designs **page 105:** *top* courtesy of Ballard Designs; *bottom* Mark Samu, design: Correia Design **page 107:** Jessie Walker, design: Kathleen McCann **page 108:** Bradley Olman **page 109:** *top* Simon Beran/Retna.com; *bottom* James Robinson/Retna.com **page 110:** *top left* Lucinda Symons/Retna.com; *top right* Mark Scott/Retna.com; *bottom* Stewart Grant/Retna.com **page 111:** *top* Mike McClafferty/Retna.com; *bottom* Winfried Heinz/Retna.com **page 112:** Stewart Grant/Retna.com **page 113:** *top* Mark Scott/Retna.com; *bottom* courtesy of Ballard Designs **pages 114–115:** Tria Giovan **page 116:** *top left* Phillip H. Ennis Photography; *top right* Mark Samu/courtesy of Hearst Magazines; *bottom right* Tria Giovan; *bottom left* Brian North/Retna.com **page 117:** courtesy of Lillian Vernon **page 118:** *left* courtesy of Elfa/The Container Store; *both right* courtesy of Lillian Vernon **page 119:** *both top* Tria Giovan; *bottom* Bruce McCandless **page 120:** *left* courtesy of Lillian Vernon; *right* courtesy of Elfa/The Container Store **page 121:** *top left* courtesy of Lillian Vernon; *right and bottom left* Eric Roth, design: Easy Closets **pages 122–123:** *clockwise from top right* Eric Roth, design: Easy Closets; courtesy of Closetmaid; Eric Roth; Mark Lohman; Eric Roth, design: Easy Closets **page 124:** *top left* Mark Samu; *top right* alanshortall.com; *bottom* Bruce McCandless **page 125:** *top* Eric Roth, design: Easy Closets; *bottom and inset* davidduncanlivingston.com **page 126:** *top* Bruce McCandless; *bottom* Jessie Walker **page 127:** *left* Pizzi/Thompson, design: Timothy Gordon, AIA; *right* melabee m miller **page 128:** *top* courtesy of All Bright Ideas; *bottom* carolynbates.com **page 129:** *right* Mark Samu, design: Susan Zogrone, California Closets; *left* Bradley Olman **pages 130–131:** Phillip H. Ennis Photography, design: Norman Michaeloff Interiors/Andrew Tedesco Studios **pages 132–133:** *both* courtesy of Plain & Fancy Custom Cabinetry **pages 134–135:** *top right* Bradley Olman; *bottom right* Eric Roth; *center* Roger Turk, design: Showplace Design & Remodeling; *bottom left* Tony Giammarino/Giammarino & Dworkin; *top left* Tria Giovan **pages 136–137:**

Eric Roth **page 138:** Tony Giammarino/Giammarino & Dworkin, design: Christine McCabe **page 139:** *right* courtesy of StoreWall; *top left* Jessie Walker, architect: Lenore Weiss Baigelman; *center left* Jessie Walker, design: Dave McFadden; *bottom left* Phillip H. Ennis Photography, architect: Opacic Architects **page 140:** *top* carolynbates.com, architect: Frederick W. Horton; *bottom right* courtesy of Ballard Designs; *bottom left* Mark Lohman **page 141:** Phillip H. Ennis Photography, design: Blodgett Designs **page 142:** *top right* Simon Whitmore/Retna.com; *bottom right* Dominic Blackmore/Retna.com; *bottom left* Bradley Olman; *top left* courtesy of StoreWall **page 143:** *top* Lizzie Orme/Retna.com; *bottom* Simon Bevan/Retna.com **page 144:** Pizzi/Thompson, design: Concepts by J **page 145:** *top* melabee m miller; *center* melabee m miller; *bottom* courtesy of Elfa/The Container Store **page 146:** *both* carolynbates.com, architect: Brad Rabinowitz **page 147:** *top both* Peter Tata, architect: Robert Steinbomer, Steinbomer & Associates; *bottom both* Peter Tata, architect: Susanna Tobin **pages 148–149:** *top right* Simon Whitmore/Retna.com; *bottom center* melabee m miller, builder: Doyle Builders; *bottom left* Jessie Walker, design: Barbara Frankel; *top left* Tria Giovan **page 150:** *left* Mark Samu, design: Lucianna Samu/Sunday Kitchens; *right* Phillip H. Ennis Photography, design: Steve Ackerman Design **page 151:** *top* carolynbates.com, design: Milford Cushman/The Cushman Design Group, Inc.; *bottom* melabee m miller, design: Lee Weissglass **page 152:** *top* Jessie Walker, design: Lydia Grabeman, LSG Designs; *bottom* Jessie Walker **page 153:** *top* Tony Giammarino/Giammarino & Dworkin, design: Nancy Thomas; *bottom right* Bradley Olman; *bottom left* courtesy of Elfa/The Container Store **pages 154–155:** *top right* Mark Samu, courtesy of Hearst Magazines; *bottom right* Tria Giovan; *bottom left* Roger Turk, design: Vision Woodworks, Inc.; *top left* Peter Tata, builder: Dave Webster; *center* Mark Lohman, design: Henry Topping **pages 156–157:** Tria Giovan **page 158:** *top right* Jessie Walker, design: Lydia Grabeman, LSG Designs; *bottom right* Tony Giammarino/Giammarino & Dworkin; *left* courtesy of Exposures **page 159:** Bradley Olman **page 160:** *top* Tria Giovan; *bottom* Pizzi/Thompson **page 161:** Jessie Walker **pages 162–163:** *top center, top right & bottom right* courtesy of Exposures; *bottom center* courtesy of Stacks & Stacks; *left* courtesy of Archival

Methods **page 164:** *top left* Jessie Walker; *top right* courtesy of Elfa/The Container Store; *bottom* George Ross/CH **page 165:** Brian Vanden Brink **page 166:** *top right* Archival Methods; *bottom & top left* courtesy of Sentry **page 167:** courtesy of Sentry **pages 168–169:** *top right & center* courtesy of Elfa/The Container Store; *bottom right* Mark Lohman; *top left* Tony Giammarino/Giammarino & Dworkin **page 170:** Brian Vanden Brink, architect: Whitten Winkleman Architects **page 171:** *top right* courtesy Rubbermaid; *bottom right* courtesy of Haier America; *top left* Eric Roth, architect: David Pill Architects **page 172:** *top* courtesy of StoreWall; *bottom* Peter Tata, design: James Carroll **page 173:** *top* Ed Reeve/Redcover.com; *bottom* courtesy of Rubbermaid **page 174:** *top right* courtesy of FrontGate; *top left & bottom left* courtesy of All Bright Ideas **page 175:** *top left* courtesy of Stacks & Stacks; *top right* courtesy of FrontGate **page 178:** Brad Simmons, stylist: ShelterStyle.com **page 177:** *top* Stickley Photo·Graphic; *bottom* courtesy of Handy Home Products **page 178–179:** melabee m miller, design: Sawhorse Designs **page 180:** *top* melabee m miller, design: Sawhorse Designs; *bottom* Mark Samu/courtesy of Hearst Magazines **page 181:** *top* Jessie Walker, design: Andrew Brown; *bottom* Tony Giammarino/Giammarino & Dworkin **page 182:** *top right* carolynbates.com; *bottom right* Eric Roth, design: Easy Closets; *bottom left* carolynbates.com; *top left* Jessie Walker **page 183:** *top* melabee m miller, architect: Karen Luongo, AIA; *bottom* Pizzi/Thompson, design: Patti Hutchins Design **page 184:** *top right* Pizzi/Thompson; *top left & bottom left* carolynbates.com **page 186:** *top* Eric Roth; *bottom* Bradley Olman **page 187:** *top left & bottom left* Phillip H. Ennis Photography, architect: Chary & Siquenza Architects; *right* carolynbates.com **page 188:** *top both* Mark Samu, design: Ken Kelly; *bottom both* Mark Samu, design: Benvenuti & Stein **page 189:** *left* Pizzi/Thompson; *right* Tria Giovan, design: Michele Prentis **pages 190–191:** *top right* Mark Samu; *bottom right* melabee m miller, architect: Studio Tagland Architects; *center* Jessie Walker, architect: Michael Lustig; *bottom left* melabee m miller, architect: Karen Luongo, AIA; *top left* Mark Samu, architect: Doug Moyer, AIA **page 192:** carolynbates.com **page 198:** Phillip H. Ennis Photography **page 201:** courtesy of Elfa/The Container Store

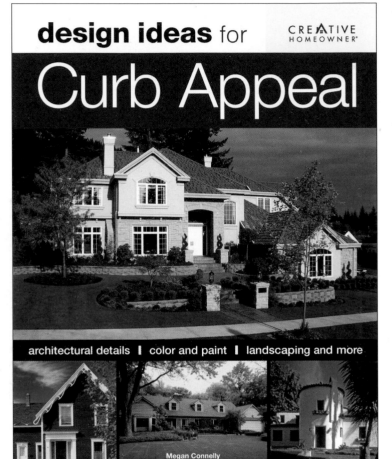